Body and Soul: Contemporary Art and Healing

ERIC AVERY

DENISE BARDOVI

NANCY BURSON

CHRISTIANE CORBAT

NANCY FRIED

ALEX GREY

MARCY HERMANSADER

KHRISTINE HOPKINS

C. REGINA KELLEY

RIVA LEHRER

TIM LOWLY

MAGGIE MCCURDY

CATHERINE NASH

DAVID SCHORR

ANN LEDA SHAPIRO

HOLLIS SIGLER

BETH AMES SWARTZ

OTTIE THOMAS-SMITH

LINDA TROELLER

body and soul

contemporary art and healing

DeCordova Museum and Sculpture Park, Lincoln, Massachusetts

Organized by Rachel Rosenfield Lafo, Senior Curator, and Nicholas Capasso, Associate Curator,
with assistance from Sarah Rehm Roberts, NEA Curatorial Intern,
and Exhibition Consultant Gina Halpern

Body and Soul:
Contemporary Art and Healing

DeCordova Museum and
Sculpture Park,
Lincoln, Massachusetts
April 23 – June 12, 1994

Samuel P. Harn Museum of Art,
University of Florida,
Gainesville, Florida
July 11 – September 5, 1994

Major support for this exhibition has been provided by the Marion R. Weber Fund of the Laurance S. Rockefeller Trust, and the National Endowment for the Arts, a federal agency.

Library of Congress Catalogue
Card Number: 93–074679
ISBN: 0–945506–15–5

Designed by Glenn Suokko
Printed by Sharp Offset Printing

Cover:
C. Regina Kelley
Quan Yin, 1993 (detail)
ceramic, 60 inches in diameter

TABLE OF CONTENTS

FOREWORD

As we approach the end of the twentieth century, individuals seek new means of relief from the stress, disease, and environmental pollution that permeate our society. Even as the federal government wrestles with the creation of a new health care system, many Americans already pursue alternatives to traditional medicine, particularly those practices that emphasize the importance of the mind/body/spirit connection.

Thus, when Gina Halpern, Executive Director of the organization Healing Through Arts, proposed an exhibition on the theme of art and healing, it seemed a most appropriate topic. Looking at ways in which artists actively engage social and intellectual issues of our society in their work has long been part of DeCordova's core mission. Indeed, as the curators conducted their research, they found that many artists from all over the United States were creating compelling artwork about illness, physical and spiritual change and growth, and healing. The resulting traveling exhibition is the first large-scale show to explore these themes, and we believe it and the accompanying catalogue will serve as important documents in the field.

The Museum is indebted to Senior Curator Rachel Rosenfield Lafo and Associate Curator Nicholas Capasso for their discerning selections and critical analyses of artists and their adept organization of the exhibition and catalogue. They were greatly assisted in their efforts by Sarah Rehm Roberts, the Museum's National Endowment for the Arts Curatorial Intern, who also authored part of the catalogue. We are all greatly appreciative of Gina Halpern's involvement as consultant. She has worked closely with the curators in shaping both exhibition and catalogue.

A project of such scope is only possible because of the generous funding of donors. The Museum gratefully acknowledges a major contribution from the Marion R. Weber Fund of the Laurance S. Rockefeller Trust and a grant from the National Endowment for the Arts, a federal agency. We are delighted to share this exhibition with the Samuel P. Harn Museum at the University of Florida, Gainesville.

Paul Master-Karnik, Ph.D.
Director, DeCordova Museum and Sculpture Park

INTRODUCTION

In April of 1991, artist and arts advocate Gina Halpern approached the DeCordova Museum to propose a national exhibition on contemporary art and healing. Halpern is a leader in the fledgling healing arts movement, and serves as Executive Director of Healing Through Arts, a national non-profit organization dedicated to exploring and strengthening the relationships between the creative arts and the healing arts through communication, education, and research. While we were well aware that certain themes of physical, emotional, cultural, and environmental healing have appeared in the work of contemporary American artists, we were unacquainted with the depth and breadth of the phenomenon that Halpern brought to our attention. We learned that themes of healing pervade not only the visual arts, but also music, dance, theater, storytelling, design, architecture and other sister arts. A grass roots movement was in the making, networked through organizations like Halpern's Healing Through Arts, and other groups including the Omega Arts Network, the International Friends of Transformative Art, Art as a Healing Force, and the Society of Health Care Arts Administrators.

Our research for "Body and Soul" placed us in contact with hundreds of artists coast-to-coast whose work deals with a vast range of issues having to do with many different kinds of healing. In order to structure a coherent and manageable exhibition, we decided to limit our focus to artists who use visual imagery and the artistic process to deal with themes of individual healing and wellness. This criterion encompasses all interrelated forms of healing which can take place for individual human beings: physiological, emotional, psychological, and spiritual.

"Body and Soul" includes four types of healing art that represent the major approaches taken by contemporary artists. These general categories often overlap within the work of individual artists:

1. *Art intended to directly heal viewers*
   These works often employ symbols or abstract images which promote wellness through a calming and centering physical and spiritual response, or activate specific physiological responses through techniques of positive visualization.
2. *Art created by artists to facilitate their own personal healing*
   These works tend to be autobiographical and involve highly-charged abstract or representational body imagery. The process of creating these works is also considered to be a healing exercise.
3. *Art about aspects of the healing process*
   These works do not necessarily perform a healing function, but comment on the pain hope, and complexities of healing.
4. *Artist-designed healing environments*
   These works, commissioned for hospitals, hospices, and other health care facilities demonstrate a new willingness on the part of the medical community to explore the healing potential of art.

It must be stressed that the artists included in "Body and Soul" consider themselves to be professional contemporary artists, not practitioners or clients of art therapy. They are united by the belief that art is life-affirming, that art can touch and stimulate healing energies, and that the creative process stands in opposition to degeneration and disintegration. They believe that art has power, not just the power of metaphor and self-expression, but a real operant power that can effect transformation, change lives, and heal. Their works are as powerful as their beliefs, and they represent not only the positive aspects of healing, but also its struggles and pain. Death, deformity, and disease appear as readily as images of health, hope, and transcendence.

The healing arts movement is the product of developments within the art world and changing conditions in health care in America. The personal, autobiographic aspect of much healing art is made possible by the rise of feminism in contemporary art, an inclusive humanistic philosophy which elevates traditional roles and concerns of women (in this case care-giving), celebrates individual experience, and places the personal on par with the political. Healing art also reflects current artistic concerns with the body and spirituality. Its active, one might say utilitarian, stance in reestablishing and maintaining health echoes the concerns of many artists today who strive to reinvigorate the arts by exploring new social, political, practical, and community applications. The creation of artist-designed healing environments in health care facilities is an important aspect of art's growing movement away from exclusive galleries and museums to a more public, and some might argue, more relevant realm.

Alternative forms of healing—practices not totally accepted by traditional Western medicine—are on the rise in this country. A report entitled "Unconventional Medicine in the United States," by David M. Eisenberg *et al.* in the January 28, 1993 issue of the *New England Journal of Medicine* revealed that over one third of Americans consulted alternative health care providers in 1990 and spent $13.7 billion in the process. The record-breaking audience for the 1992 PBS television documentary "Healing and the Mind with Bill Moyers" further demonstrates that the public is keenly interested in new approaches to health and well-being. The healing arts movement is allied with this trend, and many of the artists involved are deeply influenced by systems of healing which derive from Eastern medicine and New Age spirituality.

This exhibition catalogue for "Body and Soul: Contemporary Art and Healing" brings a number of different perspectives to bear upon the topic. Exhibition consultant Gina Halpern's essay "Healing Art: Cross-Cultural Connections," discusses the growing acceptance of the mind/body/soul wellness paradigm in both contemporary art and medicine, and finds precedence for this idea in the art and philosophies of other times and cultures. Mike Samuels, a physician and long-time advocate of the healing power of art, traces the interconnected spiritual and physiological effects of visual imagery in his visionary essay "Art as a Healing Force." And DeCordova Associate Curator Nicholas Capasso examines the recent phenomenon of artist-designed healing environments in actual health care facilities in his essay "The Artist in the Hospital." Accompanying these thematic essays are brief discussions of the work of each artist in the show by Capasso, DeCordova Senior Curator Rachel Rosenfield Lafo, and NEA Curatorial Intern Sarah Rehm Roberts.

This exhibition would not have been possible without the kind cooperation of the artists, galleries, and collectors who generously allowed us to borrow work from their collections. We would especially like to thank the Jayne H. Baum Gallery and the Mary Ryan Gallery in New York, the Sazama Gallery in Chicago, the Steven Scott Gallery in Baltimore, the Susan Cummins Gallery in Mill Valley, California, and John Ollman of the Janet Fleisher Gallery in Philadelphia.

For information on art in health care facilities, we are indebted to Lynn Basa, Director of the Art Program at the University of Washington Medical Center, Seattle; Diane Hicks (Activities Coordinator), Christine Hurley (House Administrator), and Michele Hasson (former Arts Program Coordinator) of the Bailey-Boushay House in Seattle; Topher Delaney of the San Francisco landscape architecture and construction firm Delaney and Cochran; and the Rev. Sally S. Bailey, Director of Support Services/Arts at The Connecticut Hospice in Branford, Connecticut.

Many thanks go to our essay authors, physician and healing art pioneer Mike Samuels, and artist and healing art activist Gina Halpern. Gina Halpern was also instrumental to this exhibition in her role as Executive Director of Healing Through Arts in Cambridge, Massachusetts. She originally proposed the exhibition topic, acted as Exhibition Consultant, and placed the considerable resources of her organization at our disposal. We also thank Amy Noel Wyman of the Healing Through Arts staff.

Others who have given generously of their time and advice include Beth Gates-Warren, Senior Vice President and Director of the Photographs Department at Sotheby's, New York; Linda Samuels, Director of Art as a Healing Force and Curator of the Bolinas Museum in Bolinas California (the show "Art as a Healing Force" at the Bolinas Museum in 1991 was the first thematic exhibition on art and healing); Neery Melkonian, Curator, Contemporary Arts Center in Santa Fe, New Mexico; David Floria, former Director of the International Friends of Transformative Art in Sedona, Arizona; Peter Gordon, Curator, San Jose Museum of Art, San Jose, California; Dede Young, Curator of Exhibitions, Samuel P. Harn Museum of Art, University of Florida at Gainesville; Zachary Morfogen of Morfogen Associates; Herbert Benson (Founder), Richard Dalton (Marketing Director), and Marilyn Wilcher (Program and Development Director) of the Mind/Body Medical Institute at the New England Deaconess Hospital, Boston, Massachusetts; Honey Doctoroff, Program Coordinator, On My Own Time Program, Tufts Associated Health Plans, Waltham, Massachusetts; Anne G. Arsenault, Program Planner for Interface, Cambridge, Massachusetts; and Suzi Gablik, Elizabeth Franco, Richard McCurdy, Susan Dobinsky, Rob Paral, Mary Van Cline, Judith Raphael, Phyllis Rosser, Geraldine Rosenfield, and Glenn Suokko, designer of this catalogue. Special thanks go to Marion Weber for her enthusiastic support for the Museum and the "Body and Soul" exhibition.

We would also like to acknowledge the valuable assistance of DeCordova Staff members: Director Paul Master-Karnik, Associate Director for Development Denise Trapani, Registrar Lynn Traub, Curatorial Staff Assistant Susan Atwater, Preparator Brad Gonyer, Museum Technician Peter Berry, Photographer George Vasquez, Designer Anna Holland, Public Relations Director Michael Sockol, Director of the DeCordova Museum School Eleanor Lazarus, Outreach Coordinator Carole Somol, and Curatorial Interns Sara Cassidy, Elizabeth Simmons, Caroline Vosburgh, and Penny Vinik.

— Rachel Rosenfield Lafo,
Senior Curator

— Nicholas Capasso,
Associate Curator

— Sarah Rehm Roberts,
NEA Curatorial Intern

Healing Art
Cross-Cultural Connections

Gina Rose Halpern

Healing Art is emerging today as a new field bridging the worlds of art and medicine. The roots of the relationship between art and healing go back to such questions as "Why was I born? Who brought me into this body? Why do I suffer? Why do we die?" From earliest times the essential life questions have been the same, and we turn to the heavens and to the interpreters of the mysteries for our answers. Shamans, priests, mystics and healers explored these questions through prayer, vision quests, meditation, and observation of the phenomena of the natural world. They looked deeply into our relationships with our environment, our fellow beings, and our own awesome and complex bodies. They traveled far on their journeys and brought back their discoveries, which they recorded in soul maps on cave walls and skins, and in song so that their families and communities might follow them. Over time the various religious traditions codified these first explorations into elaborate rituals and art forms. Like the early explorers who were inspired by ancient myths and stories, today's healing artists often look to the past as a source of knowledge. In their journeys along these ancient pathways of knowing, the artists make their own vital discoveries, which they add to the wisdom of the past as maps for the journey of body and soul.

In a time and culture when we have lost much of what once nurtured us in families and communities, when many of us have lost our connections to a spiritual life or religious tradition, we feel even more isolated and alone when confronted with a trauma or health crisis. The work of healing artists shows us new pathways and guideposts for our journeys towards healing, peace, and acceptance. Their images make tangible our greatest fears, questions, and hopes. While at times these images may seem too intense or frightening, they provide a framework for moving out of denial and into the power that comes with recognizing the truth of our own experience.

Artists who create work to heal others share a rich, multi-layered and symbolic language. They communicate their healing intent to the viewer or patient through the created object or painting. "May this work relieve suffering. May this work help to bring hope to myself and to all beings. May this work bring joy. May this which I create bring comfort, inspiration, and peace." This intent remains central to the artist/healer.

The power and forms of contemporary healing art have origins in many ancient cultures and among many religions. In particular, the Navajo culture, Tibetan Buddhists, and medieval Christian mystics developed sophisticated systems for the creation and implementation of art as a means of healing. These three cultures recognize the importance of the relationship among the mind, body, and spirit.

In contemporary Western society, Herbert Benson, M.D., of the Harvard Medical School, first charted the healing benefits of eastern meditation through his medical research, which culminated in his book *The Relaxation Response*. His findings led to the development of the field that we now call mind/body medicine. This field researches the roles that the mind can play in strengthening the immune system, helping to reverse cancer and heart disease, and bringing relief from pain and peace of mind to those in the final stages of an illness. The mind/body field recognizes the inter-connectedness of all the elements of our being and the impact stress has on our physical, emotional, and spiritual health. But mind/body medicine has roots in many of the same sources as healing art. In fact, until relatively recent history healing practices blended art and music with medicine and spirituality.

The Navajo emphasize an inter-connection of body/mind/spirit in their elaborate ritual healing ceremonies called "sings" or "chants." These "chants" occur over many days, combining support for the patient by gathering friends and families who join in the ritual performance of the medicine man. A skilled practitioner of spiritual and healing art conducts a ceremony of specific poetry, song, and mythology and creates a sand painting.

> Of the most numerous technical divisions of ritualistic procedure, that concerning the sand paintings is among the most unusual and interesting. It is difficult for one who has never seen the ceremony to understand why the Navajo spend hours achieving an intricate mosaic of dry colored sand, and then, after infinite pains have been taken, the medicine man immediately walks upon it, guardedly of course but nevertheless making tracks. Then ceremonial meal is sprinkled over it so that in a minute the clear delicate outlines are obliterated. The Navajo call the subsequent procedure 'using' the painting, for the patient or patients next sit upon one of the major figures. Twenty minutes after the patient and guests have been called into the hogan, one can hardly recognize the picture. To the Navajo it has become a useful thing, something beyond the purely ornamental. It represents the presence and assistance of deity, and until the sand has been gathered up in a sack and ritually disposed of, it is feared as well as revered.[1]

The Navajo healing "chant" and sand painting provide an example of a holistic approach to recovery that combines the most potent elements of treatment. The patient is supported by friends and family and receives the full attention of the practitioner. Rather than being separated from self or community by disease, the individual is united with spiritual and environmental resources that seek to restore a natural harmony and balance. The process acts as a powerful system of transformation through which the patient merges with or absorbs the healing properties of the sand painting by sitting in the center of the image (figure 1).

The Dalai Lama, spiritual leader of the Tibetan people and recipient of the Nobel Peace Prize in 1989, states:

> I believe the ultimate aim of all human beings is to obtain happiness and a sense of fulfillment. These objectives can be achieved through physical amenities and proper mental development, but the dominant and ultimate factor is the mental aspect. In order to achieve these objectives one must have knowledge about both mind and matter. Science has made tremendous progress in understanding and harnessing matter. Buddhism, on the other hand, has a profound philosophy and over the centuries has developed a systematic method

> of shaping and developing the mind. Whether we are scientists or spiritual practitioners our basic needs and aspirations are the same. Scientists may study mainly matter but they cannot ignore the human mind or consciousness; spiritual practitioners may be engaged mainly in developing the mind but they cannot completely ignore their physical needs. It is for this reason that I have always stressed the importance of combining both the mental and the material approach to achieving happiness for humankind.[2]

The Tibetan monk venerable Lobsang Samten, Director of the Chenrezig Tibetan Buddhist Center in Philadelphia and one of the contemporary creators of the ancient Kalachakra sand mandala, speaks of the artist generating the heart of "right motivation" before performing any sacred and healing art. How does one generate right motivation?— by cultivating the Buddha qualities of compassion and wisdom. These two attributes are central

figure 1
Navajo Child in Medicine Circle
Photo: Charles Herbert,
© National Geographic Society

to all forms of healing. How does one cultivate wisdom and compassion?— through awareness, introspection, and attention. How does one acquire awareness, develop an introspective nature, and learn to be constantly attentive and open to the experiences of life? These gifts come through contemplation, prayer, and meditation. These basic designs for healing are shared by many religions and wisdom traditions. They take on form and emerge in a concrete way as sculpture, paintings, and other art forms, brought to life through the eyes and hands of the healing artist.

Tibetan Buddhism advocates a specific and evolved prescription for the growth and development of the medical practitioner, healing artist, and patient. Healing, balance, and serenity are acquired through the practice of meditation and visualization so that their presence eventually transforms the individual. Sacred paintings called "tankas" that represent physical images of the Buddhas are created for use in visualization and are thought to transmit the Buddha's message of wisdom and compassion to the individual. Through daily practice of these visualizations, the Buddha's essential knowledge is absorbed into the psyche and body.

The mandala, which is usually a circular image with a central focal point, is another form of healing imagery (figure 2). The word "mandala" comes from the Sanskrit, meaning wheel. Many religions and spiritual traditions employ the mandala as a focus for prayer. C.G. Jung used the mandala as a tool in the healing process of his patients and himself. As he documented the creative healing process of his patients through their work with mandalas, he developed a cornerstone of the field of psychological work that we now call art therapy. Jung describes the traditional and personal development of mandalas for healing:

> Whereas ritual mandalas always display a definite style and a limited number of motifs as their content, individual mandalas make use of a well-nigh unlimited wealth of motifs and symbolic allusions, from which it can easily be seen that they are endeavoring to express either the totality of the individual in his inner or outer experience of the world, or its essential point of reference. The fact that images of this kind have under certain circumstances a considerable therapeutic effect on their authors is empirically proved and also readily under-

figure 2
A Tibetan Monk in Nepal creates a sand mandala to relieve suffering and bring happiness to all viewers.
Photo: Gina Halpern

> standable, in that they often represent very bold attempts to see and put together apparently irreconcilable opposites and bridge over apparently hopeless splits. Even the mere attempt in this direction usually has a healing effect.[3]

The mandala also plays a significant role in Tibetan art and architecture. I witnessed the most beautiful example of the interrelationship of the mandala and healing in a tiny Tibetan temple in the Himalayan Mountains of Nepal. A two-story structure of harmonious proportions, the temple adopts the shape of a square mandala. Tibetan buildings, particularly temples and sacred spaces, often use the mandala as a blueprint, suggesting the spiritual nature of the buildings through the architecture. A giant ten-foot tall cylindrical prayer wheel stands in the entry hall on the ground floor of the temple. Intricately carved and painted with prayers, the wheel spins on an axis perpendicular to the floor. The individual rotates the prayer wheel by walking around it clock-wise, in a meditative way. As the person circumambulates, the spinning wheel releases the inscribed prayers into the universe for the good of the individual and for the good of all sentient beings. One might call this chamber the "waiting room" or the equivalent of the western clinic, but here prayer sets the tone for both practitioner and patient. The walls of the stairway leading up to the main sanctuary are covered with brilliantly painted murals of the buddhas and other deities, so that as one ascends the stairs one receives the protection of their presence, and physically experiences oneself traveling upward to their sacred realm.

The philosophy of Hildegard of Bingen, a twelfth-century Christian abbess, mystic, artist, and healer, closely parallels the Tibetan Buddhist ideals of wisdom and compassion. Hildegard left an enormous collection of writings on medicine and spiritual philosophy. She also composed ethereal music and created a series of illuminations in the form of the mandala that are prescriptions for health, wellness and spiritual nourishment. The illuminations in her book *De Operatione Dei (On the Work of God)* closely resemble the Tibetan image of the wheel of life. Both Hildegard and the Tibetans offer diagrams of the totality of the life/death universal experience, indicating both the causes of suffering and its remedies. Hildegard of Bingen's images (figure 3) take the familiar format of Western Christian manuscript illuminations. She shows herself in the lower left corner of the painting, representing every man and woman on earth contemplating the great mysteries of being. The elements and polarities of existence, the cosmic forces that affect our lives surround the main figure at the center of the circle. The image represents awareness, wholeness, integration and health.

Another well-known healer, Florence Nightingale, wrote about the role of art and the environment on health. In her 1859 book, *Notes on Nursing: What It Is and What It Is Not,* Nightingale postulated: "Little as we know about the way we are affected by form: by color and light, we do

figure 3
Saint Hildegard of Bingen,
Man at the Center of the Universe,
Codex Latinum, 1942 c.98 r.
Biblioteca Statale, Lucca, Italy.
Courtesy of Scala/Art Resource, NY.

know this, they have an actual physical effect. Variety of form and brilliancy of color in the objects presented to patients are actual means of recovery. People say the effect is only on the mind. It is no such thing. The effect is on the body too."

Contemporary designers of health care facilities are beginning to recognize the essential role that environment plays in a patient's life, affecting both the rate of recovery and the quality of life. For example, during extended stays in a major Boston hospital, a cancer patient brought paintings, music, shells, and photographs to her room, attempting to create a home-like environment. The benefits far exceeded her initial intention, as she described: "Before I began bringing my living room to the hospital with me, I was just another disease. Nurses would often come into the room and never even make eye-contact with me. After I brought in the artwork and music, they began to notice the paintings, and ask me questions about the music. I became a person to them instead of just another illness." In her attempts to re-create her living room, she created a hospital room for living rather than dying.

Organizations such as the National Symposium on Healthcare Design and the Society of Healthcare Arts Administrators (SHAA) seek to humanize and re-vitalize health care by including the arts in design and sponsoring on-going exhibitions and interactive art programs. The medical community now acknowledges that stress, unresolved anger, and negative emotions can contribute to many serious illnesses. Doctors have moved beyond the practice of surgery and the administration of drugs to recognize that environment, changes in life-style, and work with support groups, as well as meditation and visualization, can benefit the patient.

Creating a positive healing environment affects every member of the health care community, beginning with patients, and extending to families, health care providers, and staff. The beauty of sensitive and inclusive design and art can be seen clearly in the Bailey-Boushay House, an AIDS hospice in Seattle, Washington, which involved the Seattle artist community as active contributors to the total healing environment of the facility. Artists worked with administrators, Bumgardner Architects, and interior designer, Mercedes Fernandez, to develop what Laura Brunsman described in *Reflex* magazine as "an interactive art that reaches out as an active healing agent."[4]

The emergence of patient-centered care and human need-based design, rather than just health care design for medical technological efficiency, is very encouraging. This new focus restores us to our "personhood" in basic ways, as we deal with illness and healing, as patients, family, or health care providers.

The rising growth of the fields of art therapy and other expressive therapies testifies to the effectiveness of art as a therapeutic tool for the ills of the soul and psyche. In his book *Art as Medicine: Creating a Therapy of the Imagination,* art therapist and author Shaun McNiff says "Shamanic cultures throughout the world describe illness as a loss of soul. The shaman's task is to go on a journey in search of the abducted or lost soul and return it to the sick person."[5] How do the fields of healing art and art therapy differ? In art therapy the creative act of art making (rather than the finished art work) holds therapeutic value. In contrast, while the process of creation is also important for the healing artist, the finished art work is the primary agent for healing.

Healing images derive their potency from their basis in the truth of human experience. In his painting *Dying,* Alex Grey presents us with the moment of our greatest fear. Grey's vision of the spirit "sees" our death and suffering and offers serenity and reunion with the source of light and understanding. Christiane Corbat's *Amazon, Cry for Life,* a one-breasted, armor-plated figure says, "I am not just a cancer patient, I am a survivor! I am a proud Amazon Warrior." Nancy Fried's terra-cotta sculptures hold up a mirror to the woman who has undergone a mastectomy. Her pieces boldly allow us to participate in a deep experience of shared recognition and loss. They draw us out of the isolation of our disease and remind us that we are not alone in our loss and shame and suffering. These feelings send important life-affirming messages and connect us to a source of personal and collective empowerment.

For the artist who confronts his or her own suffering, the creation of the work itself often contains a healing or therapeutic dimension. The artist also invites us to enter the soul of being and healing, a prospect that can be both confrontational and comforting. Though illness or loss may bring on a sense of isolation and alienation, the work of the healing artist reaches out and says, "See, you are not alone. I have been there too." We can be touched by the compassion and shared experience. We can also connect with the underlying power of the creative spirit that gives life to the art, to the artist, and to us.

Healing art provides us with models of identification. For some individuals the intensity of these images can be disturbing. Such reactions are part of a struggle with denial that can accompany disease and the possibility of death. But for many, the power of this art lies in its ability to connect us to ourselves. Healing art gives opportunities to see our deepest sadness and fear made visible. The articulation of unspoken pain provides us with a sense of recognition and the potential for release that is essential to recovery and serenity. Until recently, cultural and medical models in the West praised the individual who accepted pain and took medicine stoically, but now these models are changing in response to evidence that this behavior does more to impede the healing process than it does to assist us in our journey towards wholeness.

As we perceive and receive the abundant imagery of the healing artist, we are brought back from our lost soul-wanderings into the map of clarity. We are brought back into the fullness of the picture, and into the fullness of our own lives. We are no longer lost and alone. We have found the charts to guide us homeward.

Painter, sculptor and writer Gina Halpern teaches fine arts at Buckingham, Browne and Nichols School in Cambridge, Massachusetts, and conducts workshops exploring the use of the creative process as a method for personal discovery. She acts as Executive Director of Healing Through Arts, a Cambridge-based organization founded to explore the relationships between healing and the creative arts.

Notes

[1] Gladys A. Reichard, *Navajo Medicine Sandpainting* (New York: Dover Publications, 1977), p.22.

[2] From the foreword to *MindScience An East/West Dialogue* (Boston, MA: Wisdom Publications, 1991). [proceedings of the symposium sponsored by the Mind/Body Medical Institute, Harvard Medical School, New England Deaconess Hospital, and Tibet House, New York]

[3] C.G. Jung, *Mandala Symbolism* (Princeton, NJ: Bollingen, 1959), p.5.

[4] Laura Brunsman, in *Reflex: The Northwest's Forum on the Visual Arts,* volume 6, number 3, May–June 1992, pp. 8–9.

[5] Shaun McNiff, *Art as Medicine: Creating a Therapy of the Imagination* (Boston, MA, and London: Shambala, 1992), p.21.

ARTISTS IN THE EXHIBITION

ERIC AVERY

Dr. Eric Avery received a B.A. in art from the University of Arizona and an M.D. from the University of Texas Medical Branch (UTMB) in Galveston. After a residency in adult psychiatry at the New York State Psychiatric Institute, Columbia Presbyterian Hospital, he worked as photographer/artist in residence at the Hershey Medical School in Pennsylvania. In 1980, Avery moved back to his home state of Texas to live and work in the border town of San Ygnacio. His work as a humanitarian and activist has taken him to Northern Indonesia where he served as a physician on a Vietnamese refugee boat, and to the Las Dhure Refugee Camp in Northern Somalia where he served as medical director. In 1984, he helped organize the Laredo, Texas branch of Amnesty International. Currently, Dr. Avery is a fellow in the Department of Psychiatry and Behavioral Sciences at UTMB Galveston, Texas. Recent solo exhibitions include those at the Grey Art Gallery of New York University, New York; the Galveston Arts Center; The Mary Ryan Gallery, New York; and the Graham Gallery, Houston, Texas. His work has also been shown in recent group exhibitions at the Contemporary Arts Museum, Houston, Texas; the Modern Art Museum of Fort Worth, Texas; the Museum of Fine Arts, Boston; the Museum of Contemporary Art, San Diego, California, and Centro Cultural de la Raza, also in San Diego.

Eric Avery addresses ethical crises in current medical practices from a unique, double-edged perspective—he is both an artist and a practicing MD. Avery's work as a physician and psychiatrist cannot be separated from his work as an artist. His medical work fuels his art work, and his art work helps him contain and defuse the tension he experiences in his practice.

Avery works through the sadness and anger that result from daily encounters with patients and the medical system by producing artworks. His work as an AIDS psychiatrist at the University of Texas Medical Branch in Galveston generated the series of linocuts, photo-silkscreens, and monotypes he produced in the summer of 1993 during a brief residency at the Fine Arts Work Center in Provincetown, Massachusetts. The UTMB AIDS clinic appears very literally in the imagery of the prints—the leaf pattern bordering several of the prints was taken directly from the wallpaper used in patients' rooms. Avery even printed some the images on paper handmade from hospital linens. Avery's experiences in the clinic also motivate the prints on a purely personal and emotional level.

For his installation *The Stuff of Life*, Avery printed images of magnified cells from his own peripheral blood smear, the type of blood sample used for many laboratory tests, including the test for HIV. Avery printed his red and white blood cells and platelets on a series of large pieces of paper that are applied directly to wall surfaces like wallpaper. The repetitive pattern of floating cells literally surrounds the viewer in a stream of blood. Cast paper woodcut spheres of the human immunodeficiency virus hang from the ceiling in the midst of this sea of brightly colored, healthy cells. Looking both cosmic and microscopic, the virus spheres threaten the healthy blood cells, a reminder of the ever-present threat of AIDS.

S.R.R.

Eric Avery
The Stuff of Life, 1993
linocut on handmade Japanese Okawara paper, cast paper woodcut spheres
73 x 37 inches (each sheet);
12 inches diameter (spheres).
Photo: John Glowczwski

DENISE BARDOVI

Denise Bardovi has been in private practice in Los Angeles as a body-oriented psychotherapist since 1986. She teaches workshops about her techniques throughout the U.S. and Canada. Recent group exhibitions include those at the Bolinas Museum in Bolinas, California, and the Esalen Institute, Big Sur, California.

Denise Bardovi contracted cat scratch fever in February 1986. The disease destroyed her immune system, leaving her vulnerable to other infections. She then became ill with the Epstein-Barr virus which causes chronic fatigue syndrome. Her illnesses took her into a three-year battle in which she tried every weapon available to fight the virus and strengthen her immune system. During that time, she also began a series of paintings about her illness and her healing process. Although acupuncture, herbal remedies, vitamins, visualizations, and other approaches gave her some relief, Bardovi attributes her recovery to the psychological and spiritual power she gains from her paintings.

The paintings give concrete representation to the physical struggle waged within her body. Part autobiography, part metaphor, her paintings serve as an outlet for emotional pain and a forum to develop imagery for use in visualization exercises. Bardovi's complex iconography—suns, spirals, snakes, birds, feathers, flames, and hands recur throughout the series—symbolizes different aspects of her illness. Bodies within bodies illustrate the disease attacking her from the inside out. Arrows and dotted lines of energy stream through the paintings, shooting into her body and melting the disease.

In *The Shaman #2,* a snake coils around a vicious creature contained within the main figure, strangling the enemy. Two pairs of arms encircle the central figure. Their skeletal hands drip blood from the wrists, but still manage to enclose the figure in streams of energy that flow between the fingertips. A horned creature emerges from between the figure's legs, perhaps another enemy being expelled. A vein-covered hand on the right side of the image shoots electricity or blood into the central figure, fighting the disease. Yet, some of the energy veers out into the black space of the background, missing its mark.

Bardovi also incorporates Native American symbols in her imagery. Her snakes, spirals, feathers, birds, and in some instances her palette and patterning recall Native American sand paintings and other ceremonial objects. Much as a Native American shaman creates objects to cure the sick, Bardovi creates paintings to facilitate her own healing process.

S.R.R.

Denise Bardovi
#16, The Shaman #2, 1986
tempera on paper
26 x 20 inches

Denise

NANCY BURSON

Nancy Burson studied at the Colorado Women's College in Denver, and has lived and worked in New York since 1968. Recent solo exhibitions include those at the Contemporary Arts Museum, Houston, Texas; the New Museum of Contemporary Art, New York; the Museum of Contemporary Photography, Chicago, Illinois; the List Visual Arts Center at M.I.T., Cambridge, Massachusetts; and the Jayne H. Baum Gallery, New York. She has been included in recent group exhibitions at the Museum of Photography, Antwerp, Belgium, the Center for the Fine Arts in Miami, Florida, the Los Angeles County Museum in California; and the Indianapolis Museum of Art, Indiana.

Nancy Burson in collaboration with Kunio Nagashima, Program Resources, Inc./DynaCorp at the National Cancer Institute-Frederick Cancer Research and Development Center, and with art direction by Vincent Gagliostro
Visualize This, poster
(images taken with the S-4000 Scanning Electron Microscope courtesy of Hitachi Scientific Instruments), 1991,
17 ³/₄ x 29 inches.
Made possible by a grant from Creative Time Inc.

Nancy Burson is perhaps best known for her computer generated composite photographs of celebrities and politicians and for her *Age Machine*, an interactive computer that takes a photograph of the viewer and produces an image simulating how the viewer will age. More recent work includes photographs of children with cranio-facial deformities and progeria (a disease that causes premature aging in children) and another interactive computer that uses templates to produce unsettling images of the viewer as he or she would look with similar facial distortions. With these bodies of work, Burson consistently questions our society's focus on appearance and notions of normalcy and beauty and provides her audience with tools that enable them to reflect on societal conventions and issues that are often ignored or suppressed.

In 1986, responding to the illnesses of her mother and a close friend with cancer, Burson began a series of visualization images intended for use by those suffering from particular diseases. Two photographic images comprise each piece in the series—one image of diseased cells on the left, contrasted with another of healthy cells on the right. Burson created pieces for lung cancer, breast cancer, cervical cancer, leukemia, and AIDS-related pneumonia. People who are ill are encouraged to concentrate on the healthy and diseased cells to promote psychological and physical recovery.

Burson created *Visualize This* for people living with HIV. She collaborated with scientists at the National Cancer Institute to produce these highly magnified and very striking images of a healthy T-cell and a T-cell infected with HIV. HIV-positive individuals focus on the healthy T-cell and imagine/visualize their own T-cells as healthy and strong. Visualizing this desired state is thought to assist the immune system in its fight against HIV. Commissioned by Creative Time, Burson produced *Visualize This* as a poster and distributed it throughout New York City as a public art project that promoted public awareness of the AIDS epidemic and provided HIV-positive individuals with a positive tool to use in their fight against the virus.

S.R.R.

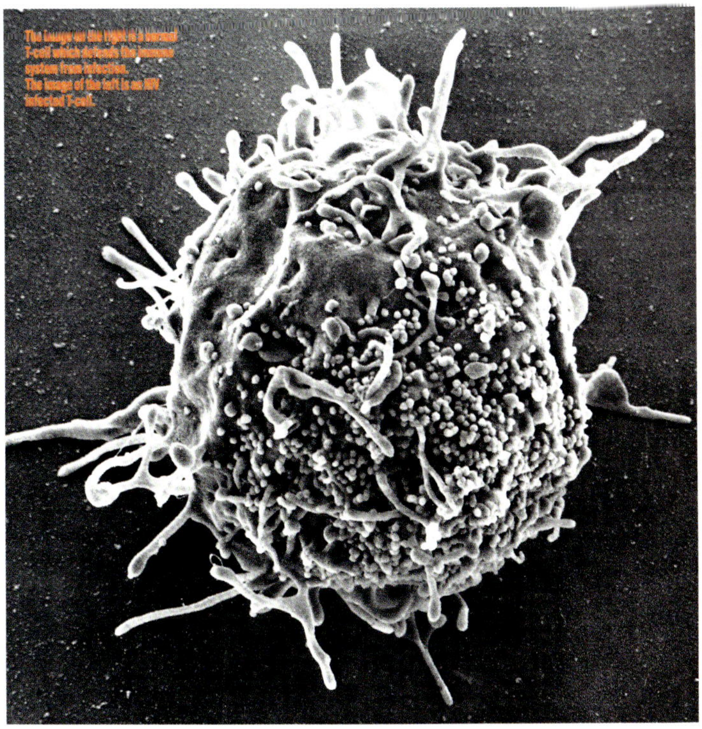

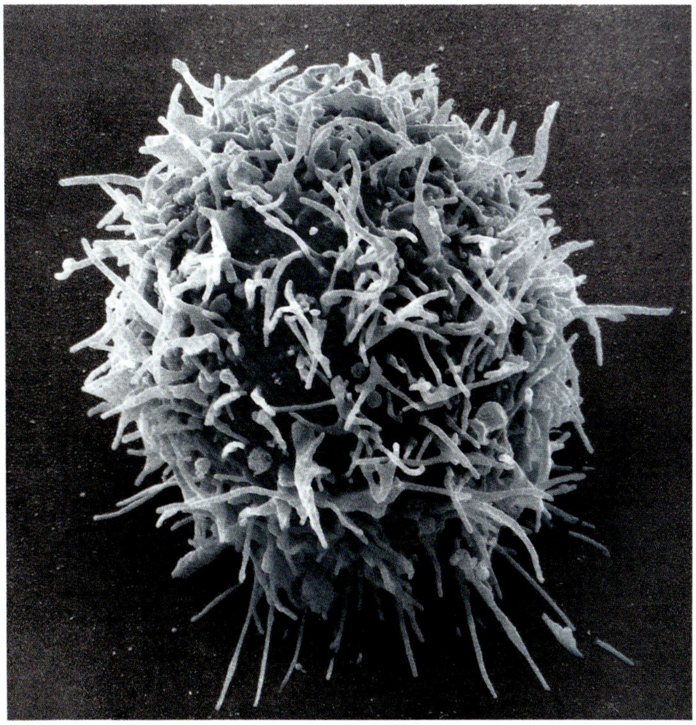

VISUALIZE THIS.

Nancy Burson in collaboration with Kunio Nagashima, Program Resources Inc./DynCorp at the National Cancer Institute–Frederick Cancer Research and Development Center © copyright 1991. Both images were taken with the S-4000 Scanning Electron Microscope courtesy of Hitachi Scientific Instruments. Art Direction by Vincent Gagliostro. Made possible by a grant from Creative Time Inc.

CHRISTIANE CORBAT

Christiane Corbat lives in Warren, Rhode Island. She received a B.A. from Sarah Lawrence College, where she studied with mythologist Joseph Campbell and art historian William Rubin. She has had solo exhibitions at the Children's Museum of Rhode Island and the Virginia Lynch Gallery, Tiverton, Rhode Island, and has been in group exhibitions at the Lyman Allyn Art Museum, New London, Connecticut, Gallery Henoch, New York City, and the Warwick Museum, Rhode Island.

Christiane Corbat
Chrysalis, 1991
mixed media
26 x 35 x 24 inches
Photo: Chee-Heng Yeong

Christiane Corbat believes that the making of a physical image can facilitate transformation, growth, and change. Consequently, in the 1980s she began making sculptures using casts of her own body to express her inner thoughts and emotions. Finding this process healing and transformational, she began to work with others who had experienced physical or emotional illness or who were seeking spiritual knowledge and growth. Her goal is to promote the well-being of an individual through the process of creating the piece: "I always tell people who wish to do a piece with me that it is *their* belief in the power of the creative act that brings about any transformation they seek, also the willingness to face their fear of change. I act as a kind of artist mid-wife."

The sculptures generally start as casts from a part of the subject's body—a torso, head, hands. Corbat then embellishes the plaster cast, adding painted designs and other materials to arrive at the finished work. Her sculptures often refer to traditions and materials used by other cultures, such as Native American, Neolithic, or Maori sources. Unusual organic materials, such as animal intestines, deer hide, and wasps' nests, enhance the mythical connections of the sculptures with the externalization of their subject's personae.

Corbat's sculptures in this exhibition refer to such issues as the sacredness of the body as a place to house the soul, breast cancer, anger, and personal loss and growth. *Chrysalis*, for example, was made with a man who was attempting to overcome great tragedy in his life. Both the title of the sculpture and its form suggest transformation and metamorphosis (a chrysalis is a form which butterflies and moths assume between the states of caterpillar and pupa). The upper part of the man's body rises from the earth, arms firmly planted and head tilted back, mouth slightly open as if in a state of acceptance and release. The wings are made of bittersweet vine and animal intestine, and the body is covered with wasps' nests and decorated in striated patterns like a Maori warrior. Corbat's sculpture effectively embodies this man's ability to overcome the darkness in his life to move toward the light.

R.R.L.

NANCY FRIED

Nancy Fried lives and works in New York, and received a B.A. from the University of Pennsylvania. Her work has been shown in recent solo exhibitions at the Graham Modern Gallery, New York, and the Joan Whitney Payson Gallery of Art, Westbrook College, Portland, Maine. She has been included in recent group exhibitions at the Kingsborough Art Gallery at the City University of New York; the Lang Art Gallery of Scripps College, Claremont, California; and the Newport Art Museum, Newport, Rhode Island.

Nancy Fried
The Flirt, 1987
terra-cotta
10 1/2 x 13 x 5 inches

Nancy Fried's sculpture focuses on the intensely personal and often very painful emotional consequences of illness. In her recent work Fried responds to the serious illnesses and deaths of several close friends. Many of these pieces use the vocabulary of small devotional altars and Mexican Day of the Dead objects. By giving three dimensional forms to the physical and psychological pain of her friends, Fried creates visual metaphors for the intangible tangle of emotions experienced by the ill and their family and friends. This recent series follows the figurative sculptures Fried produced in 1986 and 1987 in response to her own illness.

Fried's small scale terra-cotta sculptures from this period represent the complex feelings that she experienced after her diagnosis with breast cancer and her subsequent mastectomy in 1986. Some of these self-portraits express Fried's rage—*Still the Nightmare's* face twists into a furious scream. Others express profound sorrow—the figure in *Mourning* cradles her removed breast in one hand and rounds her shoulders in a gesture that looks both protective and ashamed. These works reveal the depth and complexity of the pain and anger experienced by women who have survived breast cancer and mastectomy.

In contrast, the trilogy *The Hand Mirror, Hanging Out,* and *The Flirt* offers an unexpected glimpse of another aspect of breast cancer, namely, recovery. These three figures emit a sense of self esteem and dignity. The figure in *The Flirt* faces the viewer matter-of-factly, her scarred chest bared without shame, or even modesty. Fried's figure holds the corners of her skirt in a wry, almost humorous curtsy. The straightforward modelling of the figure and the attitude of the pose suggest self-possession and a sense of confidence and ease. Fried's work portrays difficult and deeply personal thoughts and emotions honestly, but without melodrama. Her sculpture conveys the intensity of those emotions clearly and concisely, affirming the emotions of other breast cancer survivors and illustrating the magnitude of the experience for those who have not been through it.

S.R.R.

ALEX GREY

Alex Grey maintains a studio in Brooklyn, New York. He works in performance and sculpture as well as painting. He has worked as a medical illustrator and currently teaches anatomy at New York University. Grey attended the Columbus (Ohio) College of Art and Design and the Boston Museum School. He has had solo exhibitions at the University of Illinois Gallery, Normal, Carl Solway Gallery, Cincinnati, University of the Arts, Philadelphia, University of Colorado, Boulder, Islip Art Museum, Long Island, New York, Stux Galleries, New York and Boston, P.S. 1, Long Island City, New York, and at many other museums and galleries. His work has also been included in many group exhibitions. A book about his work, *Sacred Mirrors: The Visionary Art of Alex Grey*, was published by Inner Traditions International in 1990.

Alex Grey is a visionary artist whose paintings depict the spiritual journey towards self-knowledge and redemption. Relying on his own metaphysical experiences brought about through meditation, drug-induced states, and dream-visions, Grey depicts in a hyper-real style the progress of the soul through different levels of being and transformation.

His holistic vision celebrates the connections among body, mind, and spirit and the collective life of the planet. The male and female figures in these paintings are rendered with x-ray vision; their bone structures and circulatory systems are revealed to encourage us to see beyond the physical aspects of the body. Grey explains why he uses these figures without skin: "I try to press beyond our normal visual limits by presenting the interactions of the dimensions of body, mind and spirit. Mind and spirit are indicated by subtle energy emanations and sacred symbols."

In the painting, *Journey of the Wounded Healer*, we see the spiritual death and rebirth of the healer. Grey's belief that it is important to confront our own mortality came out of his experiences in the mid-seventies when he worked preparing bodies at a medical school morgue. This intimate knowledge of death combined with the artist's growing spiritual beliefs and studies of texts such as the *Tibetan Book of the Dead* led him to see the moment of death as a time of universal consciousness and enlightenment. In the painting *Dying*, death is represented not as an end but as a passage into another realm, an emanation of the spirit towards the light.

R.R.L.

Alex Grey
Dying, 1990
oil on linen
60 x 44 inches

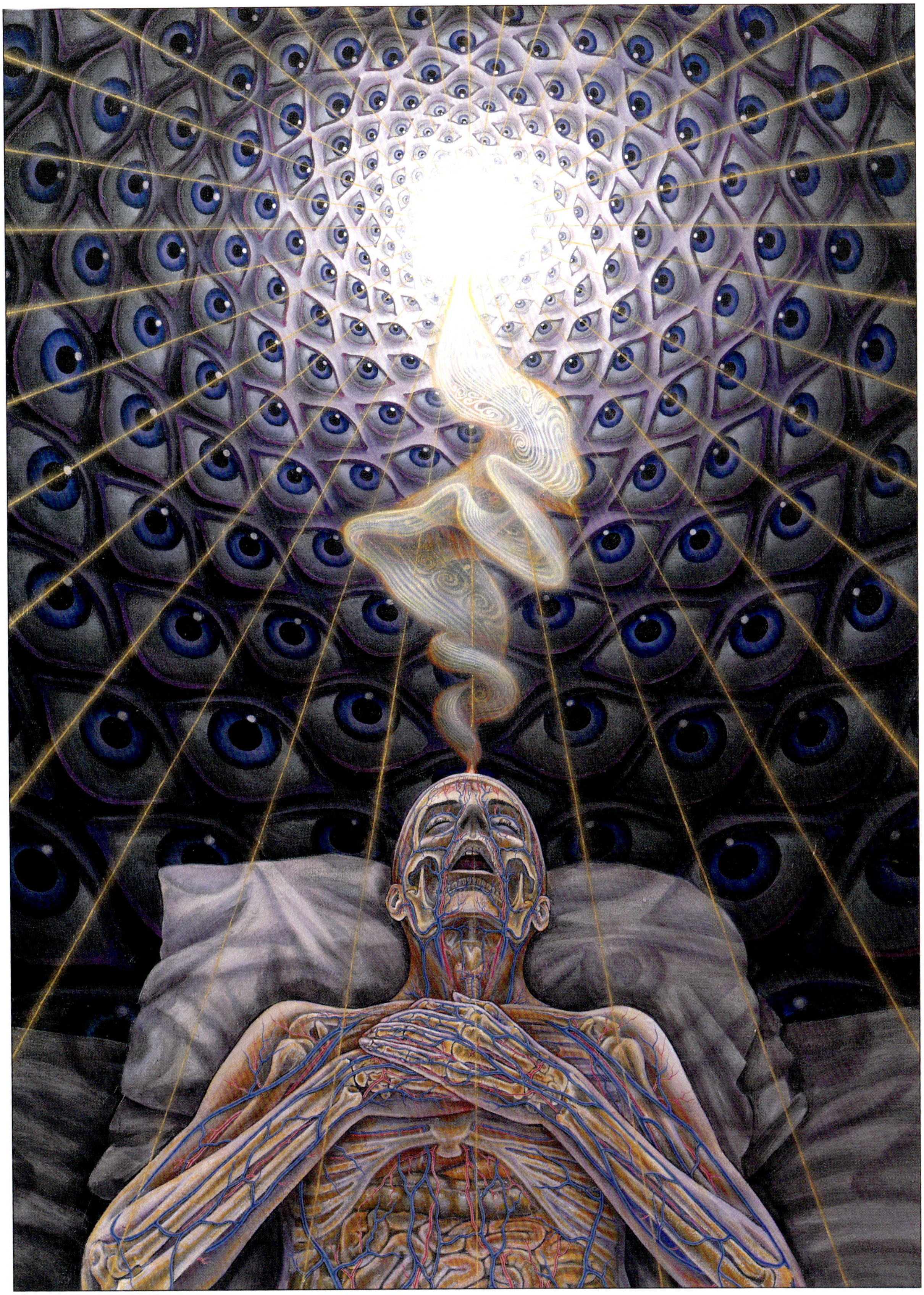

MARCY HERMANSADER

Marcy Hermansader lives and works in Putney, Vermont and has a B.F.A. from the Philadelphia College of Art. Her work was the subject of a major solo exhibition, *Belief in the Underground*, at the DeCordova Museum in 1990, and she has also had solo shows at the Williams College Museum of Art, the Cavin Morris Gallery, New York City, and the Morris Gallery of the Pennsylvania Academy of Fine Arts. Her work has been included in group exhibitions at the Delaware Center for Contemporary Art, the Philadelphia Museum of Art, Ohio State University, the Robert Hull Fleming Museum at the University of Vermont, The Bronx Museum of the Arts, and the University Gallery at the University of Massachusetts, Amherst, among others.

Marcy Hermansader's art work has always demonstrated a strong social and political consciousness. Her concerns have ranged from the poor working conditions of factory workers, to environmental pollution and disease, the exploitation of women, political oppression, and the rights of the disabled. Her subject matter became more inwardly focused, however, after she was diagnosed in 1983 with CIDP, a degenerative nerve disease.

Due to her illness, Hermansader was unable to execute her highly detailed and exactingly executed drawings, which combined color pencil, crayon, acrylic, and sometimes fabric, foil, and thread on paper. As she began to recover from the disease, she found that her entire working method had changed. Rather than carefully planning the drawings in her mind, she began to let the images develop organically, building them out of transparent layers and repeated reworkings.

Not surprisingly, the medical procedures that Hermansader experienced in the hospital became natural subjects for her drawings. Her body is presented as a theater in which dramatic alterations and transfusions of blood are enacted by enlarged blood cells, tassel-like nerves, and bones that look like ferns.

For example, in the drawing *Transfusion,* an interior landscape in which blood flows between a heart and a book, Hermansader suggests that transfusion is a metaphor for the creative process. She explains, "The intent was to suggest a mysterious occurrence taking place, like an alchemical experiment. Blood can also be a symbol for truth—blood tests can reveal invisible truths. One cannot think of transfusion and blood today without thinking of AIDS. Risk-taking, exploring the unknown, and destruction are all essential to creative work."

Fortunately, Hermansader has substantially recovered from her debilitating disease. Yet her illness profoundly affected her art and life. In her willingness to see destruction as a step in the path to rebirth, she has transformed her experience with illness into a catalyst for artistic and spiritual growth and self-examination.

R.R.L.

Marcy Hermansader
Transfusion, 1988
color pencil, spray paint, acrylic, fabric, foil on paper
31 1/2 x 39 1/2 inches
DeCordova Museum Permanent Collection
Photo: John Sheldon

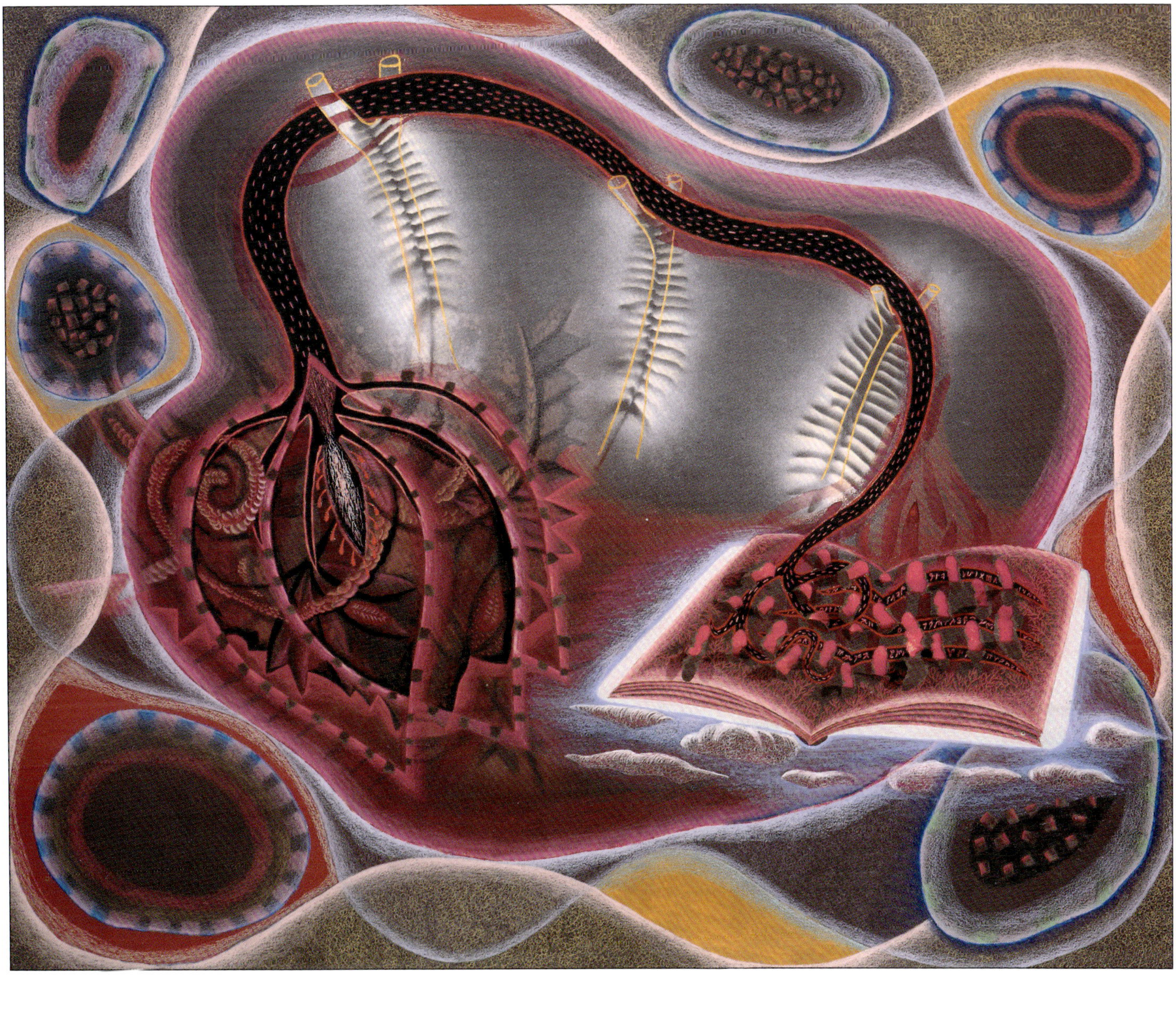

KHRISTINE HOPKINS

Khristine Hopkins lives and works in Provincetown, Massachusetts. She received a B.A. from the State University of New York at New Paltz, and attended the School of Photography at the Exeter College of Art and Design in Exeter, England. Recent solo exhibitions include those at the Boston Public Library, the Hopkins Gallery in Wellfleet, and the Hillyer Gallery at Smith College in Northampton, all in Massachusetts. Hopkins also participated in group exhibitions at the Provincetown Art Association and Museum, the Cape Museum of Fine Arts in Dennis, and the Ellen Harris Gallery in Provincetown, all in Massachusetts.

The book, *Survivors: Experience of Childhood Sexual Abuse and Healing* will be published in 1994 by Ten Speed Press, Berkeley, California.

Khristine Hopkins
#9— Yvonne, 1990
photograph hand-painted with oil paint
7 x 4 5/8 inches
and
#12— Yvonne, 1990
photograph hand-painted with oil paint
4 5/8 x 7 inches

Khristine Hopkins hand-paints her own photographs to create intimate and evocative images. The series "Survivors: Experiences of Childhood Sexual Abuse and Healing," marks Hopkins's first involvement with art as a force for healing. This set of eighteen hand-painted photographs with accompanying texts resulted from a collaborative project undertaken with seven other women, all of whom participated with the artist in a short-term therapy group for women survivors of childhood sexual abuse.

Hopkins met with each survivor to create images symbolic of a personal abuse experience and the subsequent healing process. The artist and survivor identified symbols, chose locations, attire, and props, and discussed the mood of each image. The women, including Hopkins, enact metaphorical narratives of personal transformation. After the photographs were made and painted, the women lived with the images and wrote texts about their experiences and about the artworks. From these writings, Hopkins selected passages to accompany each image in the series.

In her abuse image, Yvonne appears alone, vulnerable and terrified, in a garbage dump next to a twisted and filthy mattress. The healing image, though similarly composed, takes place on a beach, with symbols of life and regeneration. Yvonne is now literally centered, in control, and in harmony with her environment.

According to the artist, "The photographs are not graphic depictions of abuse. I'm interested in enlightening and healing rather than in shocking people. I knew that these photographs would bring up pain, for those of us in the project, and for many viewers. After bringing up this pain, I didn't want to leave people feeling hopeless. I wanted to create something that would give hope to those who are most in need of it. For me, it's the belief that healing is possible that transforms a victim into a survivor." Hopkins's "Survivors" series aided in the personal healing and growth of the artist and the other survivor-participants, and provides hope and affirmation for other sufferers of post-traumatic stress related to childhood sexual abuse.

N.C.

#9 Yvonne:
I am disembodied...split in two ...the lower half of me a woman's body, frozen, waiting for deliverance...the top half smaller, childlike, full of despair... alienated from my body, contaminated in my spirit.

#12 Yvonne:
I am sad that it has taken so much care to make this one flower open. I want to feel beautiful, and loved, and nurtured. That shouldn't be so much to want.

C. REGINA KELLEY

C. Regina Kelley lives in Portland, Maine and received a B.S. from Skidmore College in Saratoga Springs, New York, and a M.F.A. from the University of Pennsylvania. She holds the position of Professor of Fine Arts at the Maine College of Art where she teaches the courses "Healing Through Visualization and Visual Art," and "Art in Service," a course for artists who want to serve their communities. Her work has been shown recently in group exhibitions at Lincoln Center, New York City; the Southern Maine Medical Center in Portland; the Barn Gallery, Ogunquit, Maine; and the University of Maine, Orono. She has had two recent solo exhibitions at Hummingbird Arts, Cambridge, Massachusetts.

C. Regina Kelley has worked in hospice care for many years, developing visualization techniques and teaching patients methods for using art to relieve the physical and emotional pain associated with illness. Kelley also has worked with caregivers on projects aimed at helping them ease the strain of working with seriously ill patients. At the Connecticut Hospice in Branford, Connecticut, Kelley asked every staff member—from doctors to janitors to volunteers—to make a small sculpture out of wax depicting what they did to relax after a day at the hospice. Kelley and a jeweler then combined the wax sculptures into a cast bronze column. The project brought attention to the extraordinary work contributed by every member of the staff and instilled a stronger sense of community in the hospice staff. The column stands in the hospice garden as a symbol of this closely knit community and a reminder of the many ways they cope with their work.

Kelley's own art work relates closely to her interests in healing and caregiving. Her sculpture *Quan Yin* was inspired by the bodhisattva of wisdom and compassion in Chinese and Japanese Buddhism. The bodhisattva Quan Yin has undergone countless changes over the centuries, taking on various physical attributes and spiritual duties in different regions of China and Japan and in various Buddhist orders. In *Quan Yin*, Kelley refers to the Japanese tantric Quan Yin, usually depicted as a woman with one hundred or even one thousand hands. Each hand holds a different remedy or medicine, and with these, Quan Yin can cure any illness. Kelley's one hundred hands hold seven symbolic materials—corn, stars, leaves, bear claws, eyes, flames, and flowers. While some of these items have practical medicinal uses, others symbolize healing, particularly in Asian and Native American cultures. *Quan Yin* synthesizes curative and nurturing symbols from diverse cultures into a universal symbol of compassion and healing.

Kelley also has created small scale sculptures to be used as visualization objects for specific illnesses and injuries. Most recently, Kelley began a series of drawings of cells and tissue directed at coping with her own illness. She learned of her breast cancer in the fall of 1993.

S.R.R.

C. Regina Kelley
Quan Yin, 1993
ceramic
60 inches in diameter

RIVA LEHRER

Riva Lehrer lives and works in Chicago, Illinois, where she attends the School of the Art Institute of Chicago. Recent solo exhibitions include those at the A.I.R. Gallery, New York; and the Sazama Gallery, Chicago. Lehrer has been included in group exhibitions at the Elsa Mott Gallery, New York; and the Chicago Cultural Center, Objects Gallery, and Artemesia Gallery, all in Chicago.

Riva Lehrer's allegorical and narrative paintings, informed by the circumstances of her personal life, are metaphors for acknowledging and transcending life's difficulties. Her subject matter ranges from interpersonal relationships to her lesbian sexuality, to her complex medical history. The paintings, according to the artist, help her come to terms with who she is and what that means. But her work is by no means insular. Lehrer tells her stories and uses symbolism in a manner accessible to viewers. Those who experience her paintings may find affirmation of their own personal life struggles and journeys towards healing.

Lehrer's life-long struggle with spina bifida, a congenital spinal disease, provides the basis for two related bodies of work which deal with personal healing. Paintings like *In the Yellow Woods,* in which the artist is seen fashioning a new skeleton from tree branches, are symbolic, almost mystical allegories of pain, hope, and transcendence. They examine the role of the artist, the maker, as an active agent in her own healing process. Other paintings, like *Chorus,* refer directly to Lehrer's extensive hospital experience. In *Chorus,* the figure on the examination table pulls back her hospital johnnie to reveal the faces of doctors tatooed on her back and shoulders. Lehrer seems to say that a patient and her fate are literally marked by the power, influence, and personalities of health care professionals.

Lehrer's images transcend the personal because they address issues common to anyone who has experienced not only health problems, but other tragedies, epiphanies, and transformations. They speak of hope as well as pain, and acknowledge the complexities of healing. Her work also has a deep spiritual quality achieved through luminous colors, intimate scale, and in some cases hand-crafted and painted frames which act as reliquary containers.

N.C.

Riva Lehrer
Chorus, 1993
acrylic on masonite
5 x 7 inches

TIM LOWLY

Tim Lowly lives and works in Chicago, Illinois. He earned a B.F.A. from Calvin College, Grand Rapids, Michigan. Recent solo shows include those at the Kresge Art Museum at Michigan State University in East Lansing; the Grand Rapids Art Museum; the Gwenda Jay Gallery, Chicago; and the Charles A. Wustum Museum of Fine Arts in Racine, Wisconsin. Lowly has participated in group exhibitions at the Metropolitan Museum of Art and the Midtown Payson Gallery in New York; Bethel College in St. Paul, Minnesota; the Urban Institute for Contemporary Art in Grand Rapids; and the Contemporary Arts Center in Cincinnati, Ohio.

Tim Lowly paints complex allegories that rely on a wealth of art historical sources: Flemish and Italian Renaissance painting, Surrealism, and American Magic Realism. Lowly melds these influences in a personal style marked by intense color and clarity, and in an array of images marked by stillness, serenity, and silence.

One of his frequent subjects is his daughter, Temma, an eight year-old with severe multiple disabilities. Lowly paints and draws the girl with a deep love and reverence. As a Christian, he testifies to the presence of the divine in the individual in the drawing of Temma entitled *Imago Dei.* In this Image of God, however, lies a barely concealed frustration that attests to the difficulties of faith. About his daughter, the painter says, "Despite, or perhaps because of, her profound disability, she is an ongoing testimony to what it means to be 'human' and 'whole'." Lowly also sees Temma as a metaphor for the downcast in society, the vulnerable who require respect and acknowledgment rather than scorn. On a more personal level, the paintings reflect his family's psychological, emotional, and spiritual healing. They provide a means for the artist to cope with the day-to-day circumstances of Temma's disabilities, and to come to grips with the attendant spiritual implications. Lowly also hopes that his work will provide needed affirmation for others, and stimulate dialogue and awareness of the problems faced by the disabled.

In *Beacon ("Bless the Bastard"),* perhaps Lowly's most dense and multi-layered allegory, Temma lies on a mat on a pathway in an idealized landscape. She is attended by a woman who seems to bless both the child and unseen onlookers. The woman holds an olive branch and a bowl of water, a baptismal reference important in Lowly's personal iconography. To the left of the child, an enigmatic group composed of contemporary Western figures and a Korean monk (Lowly spent his childhood in Korea) build or bless or dedicate a riverside altar, shrine, or funereal cairn. While no specific and rational narrative can be deduced from this scene, the painting does yield references to the journey of life, death and transcendence, prayer and reverence, vulnerability and protection.

N.C.

Tim Lowly
Beacon ("Bless the Bastard"), 1991
tempera on panel
48 x 60 inches

MAGGIE MCCURDY

Maggie McCurdy lives in Santa Fe, New Mexico. She received a B.A. from West Virginia University and an M.A. from Southern Connecticut State University. Her work has been included in solo exhibitions at the Cloud Cliff Gallery, the Conlon Gallery and St. John's College in Santa Fe, at the Cherry Stone Gallery in Wellfleet, Ma, at the Cummins Art Center, Connecticut College, New London, and at the Davison Art Gallery, Wesleyan University, Middletown, Ct. She has been in group exhibitions in galleries in Santa Fe, Philadelphia, Chicago, and Boston. In 1975 her work was included in the DeCordova exhibition *New England Women.*

Maggie McCurdy's paintings are abstractions in which luminous surfaces are achieved through a complex process of layering materials and applying color. Upon close inspection, one can discern clusters of circular forms, often contained in a columnar shape, that are references to cell structures and spinal columns. These images are actually enlarged photocopies of medical textbook illustrations and the artist's own CAT scans and M.R.I. test results. McCurdy's inclusion of medical imagery in her art work began soon after she was diagnosed in 1987 with multiple sclerosis. Her involvement with the progress of her illness entered her paintings in a direct way; the images became metaphors for the changes taking place within her own body.

In addition to using shapes derived from pain centers in the body, cellular structure, and spinal cords, the artist also used as source material satellite images of storm patterns, because, as she explains, multiple sclerosis is like a "blizzard under the skin." McCurdy does not expect the viewer to recognize the source of her imagery; rather, she wants her paintings to be "...unknowable, yet somehow vaguely familiar." As she states it, "My search is for an art whose context is silence. This leads me to consider, then fantasize, a vast primordial realm—the soup-stuff, place of all beginnings. For me, this silent realm becomes the source space of pulsating, symbiotic forms which I attempt to glimpse, grab and freeze for observation and contemplation."

McCurdy's technique for creating her paintings is complex. Once the enlarged photocopied image is attached to the canvas, the whole is covered with acrylic medium. She uses an etching tool to incise and texture the canvas. Then shaped sections of polyurethane are applied to the surface and heated with a lamp, causing the acrylic medium underneath to bubble up. After the plastic is peeled back, creating additional textured areas, pigment is rubbed over the surface, adhering to the raised portion. Oil crayon and paint are then added. The process of layering and peeling becomes a metaphor for the layers of the body.

R.R.L.

Maggie McCurdy
Cell Stream 7, 1990
acrylic and mixed media on canvas
60 x 84 inches

CATHERINE NASH

Catherine Nash lives and works in Tucson, Arizona. She received a B.F.A. from the University of New Hampshire and an M.F.A. in mixed media from the University of Arizona. She studied printmaking in France and Vienna, and in 1987 traveled to Japan to learn wood block printing and Japanese papermaking. Nash teaches art through the Tucson/Pima Arts Council and the Arizona Commission on the Arts, and has been artist in residence for the Tucson Arts District. Her sculptural installations, prints, and mixed media drawings have been exhibited in Switzerland, Germany, Japan, and across the United States.

Catherine Nash creates environments that are conducive to meditation, healing, and protection. Prior to 1987, her art works were two-dimensional, autobiographical images that documented a personal spiritual journey. Then, acting upon her concern that Western culture separates the individual too much from the environment, she began to make three-dimensional spaces that are meant to be entered and experienced by the viewer. Nash relates this impulse to create shelters, sanctuaries, and caves to the forts that she built as a child growing up in the woods of New England.

Nash's shelters offer a total sensory experience. She uses materials such as handmade paper, pigmented wheat straw, cane, mesquite branches, stones, sand, and leaves whose textures, sounds, and smells are key parts of each installation. Controlling light effects is another important element in her goal "to provide a haven offering tranquillity and protection to soothe any inner turmoil. I hope that these environments reveal a pathway of inner focus that can enlighten one to unconditional acceptance, compassion, and love."

Nash has created a new installation, *Under Twilight's Dream,* for the "Body and Soul" exhibition. The environment reproduced in this catalogue, *Shelter: A Place of Healing,* was constructed in 1991 for the Dinnerware Artists' Cooperative Gallery in Tucson, Arizona. The piece is about the healing between Native Americans and whites and manifests Nash's interest in and knowledge of Native American culture. She has spent time with the Navajo people learning how to build sweat lodges, and many of her installations have affinities to Native American ritual spaces.

Besides creating independent art work, the artist works with different community groups on pieces that meet a specific need. For example, she received a grant in 1992 from "Healing Through Arts" to create a sculptural work with and for individuals at the Shanti Foundation, an organization that offers support to the terminally ill and their families. She has also worked with the homeless and the elderly.

R.R.L.

Catherine Nash
Shelter: A Place of Healing, 1991,
environmental installation at the Dinnerware Artists' Cooperative, Tucson, Arizona
over-beaten high-shrinkage flax pulp covering a structure of bent and lashed tamarisk branches, "forest" of mesquite branches, leaves, and other natural materials,
10 x 16 x 24 feet

DAVID SCHORR

David Schorr lives in New York, and is Director of the Studio Art Program at Wesleyan University in Middletown, Connecticut. He holds a B.A. from Brown University and a M.F.A. from Yale University. Recent solo exhibitions include those at the Mary Ryan Gallery in New York; the Davison Art Center at Wesleyan University; and the Addison Gallery of American Art in Andover, Massachusetts. Group shows include those at the San Antonio Museum; the Mary Ryan Gallery; the Forum Gallery in New York; and the Wadsworth Atheneum in Hartford, Connecticut.

David Schorr
Body, Remember, 1993
silverpoint, toned gesso with gouache and acrylic on linen
26 x 20 inches

David Schorr's recent prints and paintings deal with death and the AIDS pandemic. In 1991, Schorr began a series of lithographs which combine images of nude men and skeletons with poetic texts. Rendered as youthful, virile, and beautiful, the men fall (or float) across the surfaces of the prints in ambiguous poses which suggest agony and ecstasy, love and death, comfort and discomfort. Sometimes they hold, and are held by, skeletons in sexual embraces. For Schorr, the skeletal beings refer both to the Mexican Day of the Dead celebration and the medieval *Totentanz* (dance of death) seen in the woodcuts of Holbein and others. The accompanying texts quote romantic musings on death. For example, the lithograph *Dance of Death* includes these lines from Oscar Wilde:

> *Then turning to my love I said*
> *The Dead are dancing with the dead*
> *The dust is whirling with the dust*
> *But he, he heard a violin,*
> *And left my side and entered in.*
> *Love passed into a house of lust.*
> *Then suddenly the tune went false;*
> *The dancers wearied of the waltz.*

In a subsequent series of paintings, with figures drawn in silverpoint against delicate washes of color, Schorr extended the theme. He gradually eliminated the skeletons in favor of the elegiac men on the cusp of life and death, and expanded his range of textual inspiration and quotation to include modern, classical, and folk writings. These poetic and musical texts, which range from Aeschylus to Auden to Negro Spirituals, treat the emotional and spiritual complexities of dying, death and mourning.

Schorr's prints and paintings provide catharsis for the artist and a community of friends who have spent over ten years acting as nurses, giving care to caregivers, attending bedsides and funerals, and mourning lost loves. The works posit the full sexual vitality of life against the tragedy and transitions of death and grief in rich, intelligent, and moving dialogues. Schorr's images are healing for the artist, and healing for the caregivers, if not for people with AIDS whose loss they mourn.

N.C.

ANN LEDA SHAPIRO

Ann Leda Shapiro lives and works as an artist and acupuncturist in Seattle, Washington. She earned a B.F.A. from the San Francisco Art Institute, and a M.F.A. from the University of California, Davis. She has taught studio art at the University of Texas, Austin; the University of Arizona, Tucson; and the University of Colorado, Boulder. Her solo exhibitions include those at the Rancho Linda Vista Gallery in Oracle, Arizona; the State University of New York at Purchase; the University of Colorado, Boulder; and the Whitney Museum of American Art, New York. Group shows include those at Seattle Pacific University; the University of Texas, Austin; and P.P.O.W., 55 Wooster Gallery, and the Bess Cutler Gallery, all in New York.

Ann Leda Shapiro's artistic interest in understanding the energies of the human body led her to pursue a second and concurrent career as a certified acupuncturist. For many years her work has explored the forces which operate within, emanate from, and impact upon the human body. Originally, Shapiro's understanding of these forces was intuitive, until a thirst for greater knowledge caused her to undertake studies at the Northwest Institute of Acupuncture and Oriental Medicine in Seattle, Washington. The Eastern approach to medicine, with its focus on wellness as a balance and connectedness of bodily energies (called *qi* or *chi*), set Shapiro's subsequent course as an artist and healer.

As an acupuncturist, Shapiro explains, "Each human being is seen as a world in miniature. The practitioner and patient work together to cultivate health. The focus of the treatment is to balance and harmonize: weaknesses are toned, congested channels are opened, excesses are dispersed, tightness is softened, agitation is calmed, heat is cooled, cold is warmed, dryness is moistened and dampness is drained."

Her artworks are metaphors for this philosophy of balance and connectedness. *Intestine,* for example, is not a literal depiction of a human digestive organ. Shapiro considers the intestine not as an object, but as a process, a dynamic interface between matter and energy, linking the body to the world. She transforms the organ into a visionary image of wellness, where microcosm and macrocosm are linked by psychic and physical energies. This spiritualized landscape melds the solid, the liquid, the gaseous, and the metaphysical in nested structures. Its compartmentalized, swirling forms relate to the body's interior cellular and atomic structure, and to its exterior—the earth and the universe. *Intestine* is a meditation on wholeness, an affirmation of health and healing.

N. C.

Ann Leda Shapiro
Intestine, 1992
watercolor
24 x 36 inches

HOLLIS SIGLER

Hollis Sigler received a B.F.A. from the Moore College of Art in Philadelphia and a M.F.A. from the School of the Art Institute of Chicago. She lives in Prairie View, Illinois and has taught at Columbia College in Chicago since 1978. Her work has been shown in solo exhibitions at the Southwest Craft Center, San Antonio, Texas; the Steven Scott Gallery, Baltimore, Maryland; the Susan Cummins Gallery, Mill Valley, California; and the Akron Art Museum, Akron, Ohio. Her work has also been shown in recent group exhibitions at the National Museum for Women in the Arts, Washington, D.C.; the Munson-Williams-Proctor Institute, Utica, New York; the Center for Creative Studies, Detroit, Michigan; and the Corcoran Gallery of Art, Washington, D.C.

Hollis Sigler
Maybe It Was in Something I Ate?, 1992
oil pastel on paper with painted frame
34 x 29 inches
Photo: Michael Tropea

Hollis Sigler's "Breast Cancer Journal: Walking with the Ghosts of My Grandmothers" chronicles the artist's experience with cancer. The series illustrates the complex emotional effects of dealing with cancer and addresses how societal attitudes towards women, beauty, and illness affect the ways that women with breast cancer cope with their disease.

Outraged at the lack of funding for breast cancer research and sickened at the societal fixation on breasts that causes women to refuse life-saving mastectomies rather than lose part of their "femininity," Sigler juxtaposes her images with disturbing statistics on breast cancer and intensely personal accounts of her own thoughts about her illness.

In *Maybe It Was In Something I Ate?*, a delicately drawn chair stands alone in the middle of an empty room. Like the thought balloons that appear above the heads of cartoon characters, five ovals containing representations of possible causes of cancer float above the chair. The anthropomorphic chair seems to ask if perhaps junk food, alcohol, high power lines, or pollution caused the cancer. The imagery and Sigler's title question her role in the illness. The text painted around the edge of the frame elaborates on this fear:

> The guilt of responsibility- could I have wished this on myself? In this culture, which places so much emphasis on the individual, it is seen as a personal failing if one has a disease. What did I do that was wrong? Can I make it right again?

The spacer between the drawing and the frame offers evidence that lifestyle and/or environment must play a role in causing cancer:

> Because Japanese women have one of the lowest cancer rates in the world (especially for breast cancer), it was felt until recently that they had inherent racial resistance. But now we know that Japanese women living in the country for ten years or more have a breast cancer rate equal (to) that of U.S. women.

Sigler's work expresses a complicated web of guilt, blame, anger, and fear and speaks honestly about the stark realities of serious illness.

S.R.R.

BETH AMES SWARTZ

Beth Ames Swartz lives and works in New York City, and Scottsdale, Arizona. She earned a B.S. from Cornell University and a M.A. from New York University. Recent solo exhibitions include those at the E.M. Donahue Gallery, the Jewish Museum, and the ACA Gallery, all in New York; the University of Arizona Museum of Art in Tucson; the Elaine Horwitch Galleries in Palm Springs, California; and the Colorado Springs Fine Arts Center, Colorado. Swartz was included in group exhibitions at the Bolinas Museum in Bolinas, California; the Women's Building in Los Angeles; and the White Light Gallery and the Newhouse Center for Contemporary Art, both in New York.

Beth Ames Swartz has for many years been in the forefront of the growing healing arts movement in America. Her artwork—paintings, objects, and performances—has consistently explored personal spiritual transformation and the healing potential of ritual and image. As an advocate for healing art, Swartz lectures extensively, organizes artists' conferences and symposia, and in 1988 helped found the International Friends of Transformative Art, a healing arts organization and network.

Swartz's *A Moving Point of Balance* is her *magnum opus.* She created this multi-media installation as a healing environment, a purifying ritual based on a psychic and psychological progression. At the beginning of the sequence, viewers enter a darkened room containing a quartz polarized light and a Native American medicine wheel. This room acts as a place of preparation, a spiritual border between the profane outer world and the sacred space of the installation. Viewers next encounter a series of seven paintings based on the seven chakras. According to a 10,000 year old Tantric yoga tradition, the chakras are points in the body where matter and energy connect. The maintenance of a balanced flow of energy in and among the chakras is a key to health and well being. Each painting contains relevant abstract and symbolic imagery intuited by the artist, and is accompanied by a colored bath of light. For example, *Chakra #1* symbolizes the chakra located at the base of the spine between the anus and the genitals. Its energies are base, of the earth, involuntary and life-preserving. Its symbolic color is red. Viewers stand before the painting in a red pool of light, contemplate the image, then move on through the other chakras, experiencing and meditating upon their energies. At the end of this journey, viewers enter a culminating balancing room where they behold an ever-changing light painting of projected abstract shapes.

Swartz sees *A Moving Point of Balance* as a catalyst for healing through its mystical and symbolic resonances, its meditative and relaxing qualities, and its sensual and emotional stimuli.

N.C.

Beth Ames Swartz
Chakra #1—Base of the Spine from "A Moving Point of Balance," 1983
gold leaf and mixed media
on linen
84 x 84 inches

OTTIE THOMAS-SMITH

Ottie Thomas-Smith has a B.A. in sculpture from the Rhode Island School of Design in Providence, Rhode Island. She served a four-year internship at the Veterans Administration Prosthetic Research Center in New York, New York, and is a member of the American Anaplastology Association. She is currently President of Boston Ocular Prosthetics, Inc., with offices in Brooks and Portland, Maine, and Boston, Massachusetts.

The work of Ottie Thomas-Smith reveals the healing potential of art most starkly. Thomas-Smith, originally trained as a figurative and portrait sculptor, turned her considerable talents to a direct medical application. As a maxillo-facial prosthetist, she constructs, sculpts, and paints artificial eyes and facial parts. Made of implantable silicone, acrylics, and pigments, these parts are attached with adhesives or slipped under folds of existing tissue. Her clients have suffered massive tissue loss caused by cancers, deforming surgery, gunshot wounds, or congenital problems which cannot be addressed by plastic surgery.

Her healing work blurs boundaries between art and life, art and medicine. She takes the artistic skills of sculptural casting, three-dimensional representation, and trompe-l'oeil painting to obsessive, although necessary, extremes. In order to heal, her art must mirror life—with absolute accuracy and precision. She observes nature closely, at the level of minutia, in order to convincingly render wrinkles, freckles, broken blood vessels, and hairs. Often, Thomas-Smith will spend up to eighty hours replicating a single nose.

Ottie Thomas-Smith changes lives, and for some, makes life possible. Vast emotional healing takes place as her clients resume their daily round of activities and interpersonal relationships. Physical healing occurs when the prosthetics save lives—without the promise of safe and convincing artificial body parts, many patients would prefer death over radically deforming, albeit lifesaving, facial surgery.

N.C.

Ottie Thomas-Smith
Facial prosthetics, 1993–1994
silicone, acrylic
12 x 18 inches overall

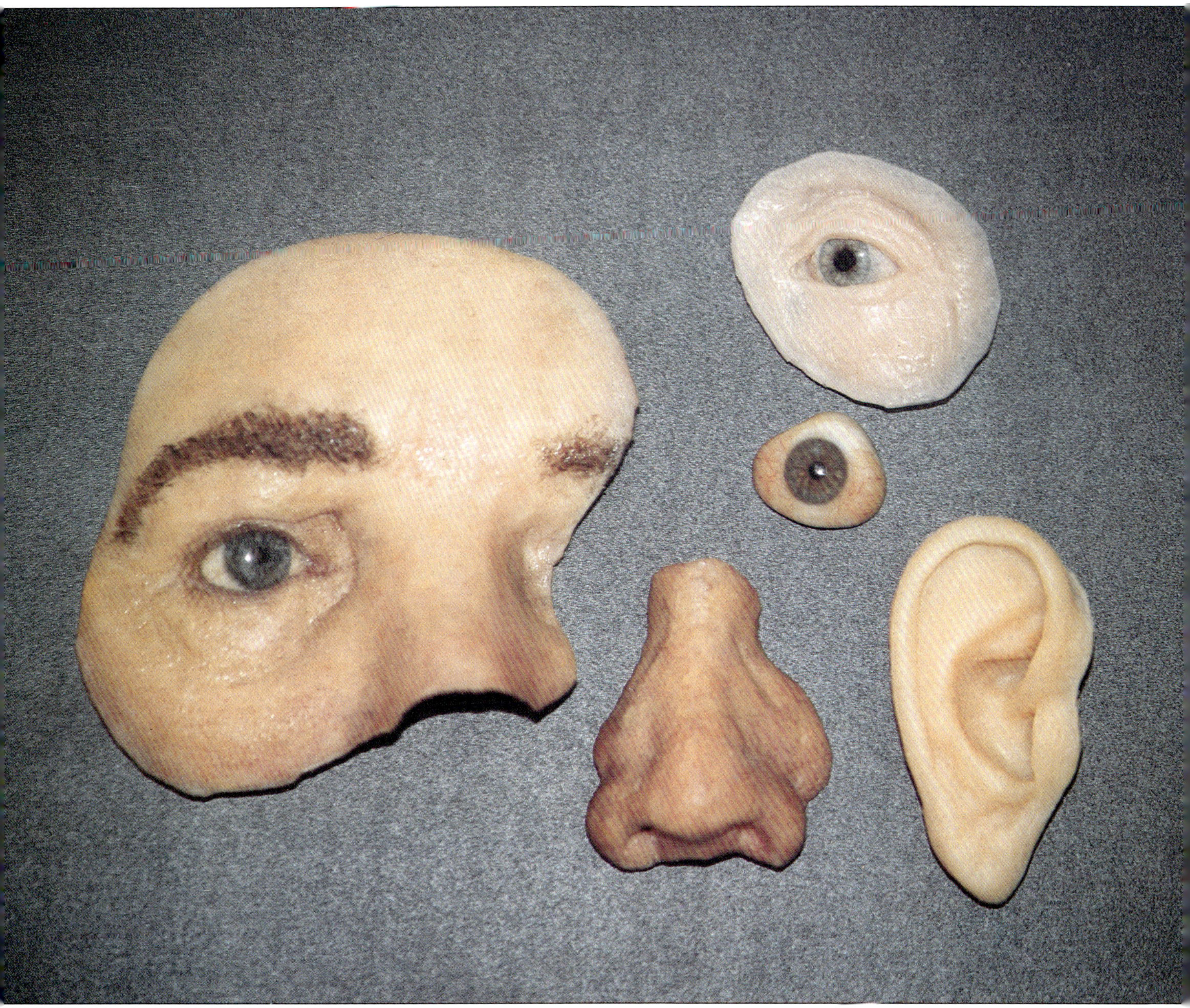

LINDA TROELLER

Linda Troeller lives and works in New York City. She has an M.F.A. and M.S. from Syracuse University, and a B.A. from West Virginia University. She has taught at the University of Nevada, Stockton State College, and Indiana University. Her photographs have been shown in numerous exhibitions in the United States, Europe, South America, and Japan. Her series "TB–AIDS DIARY" has been the recipient of numerous awards and grants.

Linda Troeller
Mud, Dead Sea, 1990
Type C print
20 x 24 inches
Photo: George Vasquez

Linda Troeller's careers as a photographer and photojournalist have led her to investigate many subjects, among them people with tuberculosis and AIDS. Her most recent series, "Healing Waters," was inspired by her own need for emotional and spiritual regeneration. Troeller began her journey to hot springs and spas around the world in 1976 when the painter Leonora Carrington recommended that she visit the Ixtapan Hot Springs in Mexico.

Troeller's travels to healing waters in places such as Belgium, France, Germany, Italy, Ireland, Japan, Israel, Cuba, Jamaica, and different parts of the United States, confirmed for her the pervasiveness in many cultures of water as a source of healing and regeneration. As she writes, "Healing water processes—baths, modern high-tech showers, drinking, rites at holy wells—provide a chance to use water intimately for relief and transformation."

Spas have been used for medicinal purposes since the times of the ancient Greeks and Romans, and have continued to be popular with those who seek healing. Troeller's research indicated that spa usage has increased considerably, which is not surprising given the public's growing interest in alternative medical practices such as hydrotherapy. Her photographs both celebrate the salutatory effect of the waters and remind us of the need to preserve their purity.

Troeller's grainy color photographs visually capture the spirituality and sensuality of the healing waters. At the Calistoga Hot Springs, a woman floats in water, becoming one with the fluid as her figure is illuminated by a warm glow of light. Steam, an apt metaphor for transformation, surrounds a man's torso and head at Carson Hot Springs, causing his form to radiate with light and energy. And at the Dead Sea in Israel, a dancer returns to the mud baths year after year, in an effort to stay young. As Troeller describes it, "He covers himself with mud....scrubs and sheds old dead skin along the shores of the sea. He rubs the natural rock salts on arms, legs, face, and torso. The shedding process draws blood to his skin's surface; a ritual which both eliminates toxins and frees young layers of skin. He continually reclaims his body."

R.R.L.

figure 1
Mary Ann Peters, *Surgery Quiet Room,* 1993, University of Washington Medical Center, Seattle, Washington

The Artist in the Hospital

Healing Environments in Health Care Facilities

Nicholas Capasso

During the late 1980s and early 1990s, contemporary artists and progressive health care administrators joined forces to create the first artist-designed healing environments in actual health care facilities. These environments—rooms, gardens, places for meditation, waiting areas, lobbies, hallways, solaria, and total design schemes—humanize and enliven once-sterile and often uncomfortable institutional spaces. Their designers and advocates believe that visual aspects of the human environment can promote wellness, and have a strong faith in art's potential to affirm life, reduce stress, and provide a focus for the emotional and spiritual energies necessary for healing.

Artist-designed healing environments exist not only for patients, but also for staff and visitors. They are places of contemplation, refreshment, and escape from glaring fluorescent lights, endless featureless hallways, and frightening medical hardware. They provide home-like havens for patients and their families, and a pleasant work environment for employees.

Health care administrators aware of the healing power of art often provide multi-dimensional arts programs in their facilities. Healing environments take their place alongside permanent or loan collections of contemporary art (real, vital, and challenging art—not posters, reproductions of old art historical chestnuts, or paintings of banal or saccharine subjects) hung in public spaces and patient rooms, displays of patient-created art, adult and pediatric creativity programs, field trips to cultural events, and traditional art therapy.

The University of Washington Medical Center in Seattle integrates art with its medical facility in three ways: a permanent collection of artwork by contemporary artists from the Northwest region hung in hallways and work areas, an artist-in-residence program involving group and individual bedside creative projects, and what program director Lynn Basa refers to as "total concept environments." In 1992, Seattle artist Mary Ann Peters created the first of these healing environments—the Surgery Quiet Room (figure 1). This room, used for intimate consultations between doctors, social workers, clergy, and families of patients, was formerly a nondescript closet-like space. Peters transformed the room with a total design concept involving furniture, lighting, flooring, and wall treatment. The now warm, inviting, and humanized Surgery Quiet Room also includes healing symbols painted directly on the walls. These include a feather (a Native American symbol of power), a flower (symbolizing birth and rebirth), and an endless knot (indicative of the web of life and the unraveling of difficult questions). According to Basa, the University of Washington Medical Center bases its Art Program on the belief "that art contributes to healing by providing a stimulating link to the world outside, and to the life force within that is reaffirmed with every artistic effort."

In 1993, Topher Delaney of the San Francisco landscape architecture and construction firm Delaney and Cochran designed the Marin Cancer Institute Healing Garden in

Greenbrae, California (figure 2). This atrium garden, built within an existing facility, can be seen through glass curtain walls and entered from the radiation area waiting room. Patients have direct access to this lush green meditative space composed of plants, rocks, and a fountain. The plants include the flowering species digitalis, echinacea, violets, and passion flowers, and also plants that are sources of cancer treatment pharmaceuticals. A brochure made available to each patient documents each of these plants with explanatory texts and beautiful black-and-white photographs by Marion Brenner. The text for the Madagascar periwinkle (*Catharanthus roseus*) reads:

This plant exhibits many healing alkaloids. The principle derivatives are vinblastine sulfate, sold as Velban used for the generalized treatment of Hodgkins disease, and vinaristine sulfate, sold as Oncovin and used in the treatment of leukemia in children. To produce one ounce of either drug, sixteen tons of periwinkle are required. The plant is primarily cultivated by the Eli Lily Company in McArthur, Texas.

In this way, patients are directly connected with the sources of their healing. The garden also advocates the healing of the biosphere necessary to maintain the biodiversity which yields cancer-fighting plants.

Topher Delaney was particularly attuned to the therapeutic needs of cancer patients, for she had battled the disease herself. According to Delaney, "This medical event transformed my own personal narrative to one of investigation of the causal relationships of art and nature which contribute to the healing of mind, body, and spirit within the framework of medical facilities." In 1993 the Marin Cancer Institute Healing Garden was awarded first prize by the National Symposium on Healthcare Design for its "innovation, aesthetic value, and contribution to life enhancement in a healing environment."

The Bailey-Boushay House in Seattle, Washington, is perhaps the most thorough instance of the integration of art within a health care facility. Built by the non-profit organization AIDS Housing of Washington, the Bailey-Boushay House opened in 1992 as the first nursing facility in the United States planned, funded, constructed, and staffed to exclusively meet the needs of people living with AIDS. This hospice has thirty-five private rooms, and serves 250 people each year, with an average residency of six weeks. Bailey-Boushay also maintains an adult day health program for members of the community who live with AIDS but are still able to attend to some daily needs at home.

Art plays a central role at the Bailey-Boushay House. An Arts Committee participated in the design process, and identified opportunities for direct physical integration of artwork in the building. The resulting architectural program allowed for artist participation in the design of the entryway, lobby area, solaria, meditation room, and garden. Moreover, twenty-five architectural wall niches were created for resident rooms and corridors. Each niche contains the work of a different artist, chosen from a pool of 144 applicants. The artworks reflect various cultures, styles, and concerns, and range from painting and sculpture to mosaics, altars, constructions, and calligraphy. Many are interactive. They contain moving or rearrangeable parts, or allow residents to add their own elements. The symbology and imagery in the niches are, for the most part, meditative, decorative, playful, dreamlike, or spiritual.

About his contribution to the niche project (figure 3), artist Mark Calderon explained: "My goal...is to create a quiet place for reflection. After much thought I decided to create a niche inspired by some of the Catholic *nichos* I have seen in Mexico. I started off by plastering the inside of the niche, then painting and 'weathering' the surface. In the center is a lead relief with the image of an abstracted torso/heart that is stitched up the middle—a personal image of healing. Below is the name plate "Milagro," which in Spanish means miracle....In the lower left is a small red glass vase for flowers. On the right is a religious object from Mexico also used in prayer. I tried to create a niche that would be a source of strength by including some of the things that are powerful to me."

The Bailey-Boushay House also displays loaned artwork in hallways and public rooms, and provides patients with an art therapy program (along with individual and group counseling,

figure 2
Topher Delaney of Delaney and Cochran, *Marin Cancer Institute Healing Garden,* 1993, Greenbrae, California

spiritual counseling, psychiatric care, and nutritional counseling). This holistic approach to the end of life's journey, with art as a central component, provides a place of profound respect and dignity for residents, their loved ones, and staff.

The roots of the trend towards artist-designed healing environments can be found in both the art world and the health care industry. Contemporary artists have been increasingly eager to re-invigorate art, to embark on projects more socially pro-active and meaningful than the creation of images and objects for display in galleries and museums. To this end, painters, sculptors, photographers, printmakers, *et al.* have moved increasingly into the public realm to harness their particular skills to social agendas, to provide interactive experiences for viewers, to collaborate with organizations outside the traditional art world, to re-invest art with a profound societal function. The healing arts movement, based on an awareness and direct application of the power of art, reflects these tendencies.

Doctors, nurses, and hospital administrators, designers, and architects have become increasingly aware of the healing qualities of art. The successes of art therapy, the lessons learned from visually and materially enlivened pediatric spaces, and the widespread influence of the hospice movement (which above all else stresses respect and comfort for patients), as well as increasing demands by patients for improved health care environments, have combined to foster a new climate of acceptance for art, artists, and the idea of wellness through design. A number of fast-growing professional organizations, including the Society of Health Care Arts Administrators, the National Symposium on Health Care Design, and the International Arts-Medicine Association now advocate the incorporation of art in health care design. Furthermore, companies like Creative Connections and The Aesthetics Collection, Inc. serve as consultants to hospitals, doctors' offices, and nursing homes which seek to build arts programs and healing environments. As the twenty-first century approaches, and as holistic approaches to healing become more widespread, artist-designed healing environments will continue to proliferate in health care facilities.

figure 3
Mark Calderon, *Niche,* 1992,
mixed media
for the Bailey-Boushay House,
Seattle, Washington

Art as a Healing Force

Mike Samuels, M.D.

Art, prayer, and healing all come from the same source, the human soul. The energy that fuels these processes is the basic force of life, the force of creativity, of love. It is nothing less than the spirit soaring, relaxing, expanding, growing. Deep within us we have memory of the beautiful place where our spirit was given breath. We know the beginning, God. We are connected to its soul in the deepest marrow of our being. Far within, I believe, are the deep spaces, the furthest reaches of the soul. They are connected to the source by a bridge, one so narrow and steep that we can only reach further by disappearing and reforming again on the other side. By traveling inward we can glimpse these worlds, feel them, live in them. And we can bring back their memory traces, bring back their spirit, only with art.

For I believe that the voices of the inner worlds speak to us in a language that, in our world, is most similar to art. It is below words, it is above silence, it is closest to poetry and music. It is God singing. It is our soul listening. It is the voice of the life force, of expansion, of love, within us. It is the connection, the real bridge, the source of all power. And when we pray, when we travel inward and heal, we can bring back traces of the pure spirit. These footprints are art. Art is the voice of the spirit. Art is the energy of healing.

So I believe that art and healing are sisters. They are tied together with a silver thread, they are bound irreversibly through time. Only in the entrance to the timeless spaces do the ties unbind, and there, all are one, the each, is.

Today the artist and the healer feel the rebirth of the ancient connection. The first artist and the first healer was the shaman. The shamans traveled inward, glimpsed the spirits, acted, brought back the healing, and made art. They told the tale, crafted the masks, danced the song, brought the inner world outward as plastic art. Now in an age when art has become decorative and lost its meaning, in an age where medicine has lost its connection to the heart, art and healing must be reunited.

If the force is love, and the voice the soul, and its language art, and its product healing, where are we going? How does art come into the medical center, healing come into an artist's studio? With awakening comes rebirth. With death and emptiness, an opening of the heart. And art and healing fill that opening. Into the heart of the artist yearning for meaning comes healing. Into the heart of the healer looking for meaning, emotion, and a language, comes art. And art becomes the doorway into the realm of the heart. Art is the tool for transformation that we now seek. It is that which opens and that which changes. When a patient in a cancer ward is visited by an artist at the bedside, and lets him or herself move into the other land, and lets a piece of art come out into the world, and then cries and is touched for the first time since he or she has been in the hospital, a healing has taken place. We have reached the place of return, the enchanted place of openness, feeling, emotion, and release. We have opened our hearts to love.

So art is a doorway, the vehicle by which an open heart can enter medicine. And medicine as an invitation, a reaching out, a need, draws artists in and lets them love, too. For in love we need a lover and a loved one, in healing we need a healer and a person who needs healing, and here, the bridge between them, the invisible connection is art, the language of love.

How does art heal? From a medical point of view, from a spiritual point of view? How can an image change reality? How does looking at an image change our body's physiology? We are just beginning to feel and understand what is happening here, and as usual, our understanding is the most concrete as it approaches the body. Western medical science has explanations for healing that are rational and testable through the scientific method of experimentation and randomized studies. That makes us feel that the explanations are true and meaningful. But in the realm in which we are traveling, this is only the surface. Art, of course, is way beyond the scientific method, and resides far in the reaches of the soul where the psychologist barely goes. So where should we start? Shall we go from the body backwards, ground ourselves, if you will, with flesh, or shall we begin with the source, from the farthest reaches and come back out? I will tell the story from my viewpoint, from inside out.

At the source we are all connected. We are one and our souls touch. There, in the place of the birth of the deepest images we can sense, is a universal land, a land of awesome power and beauty. From it come paintings of stars, of swirls, of light, of radiance. From that realm comes expansion, movement, the first life, the softest sounds. The sounds of silence, the *om.*

And closer to the surface we find the shimmering lights, the radiant colors, the movements, the birth of forms. From this world come the bright paintings, the chimes, the rising—all abstract to say the least, but full of the energy of life.

And in the next worlds we see the birth of symbols, the lands of the peaceful and wrathful deities, more familiar to us than the deeper realms, as familiar as our dreams, our nightmares. From here come dream figures, animals, snakes, flowing energy, guide figures. From here come many of the images of surrealist art, the images of myth, the new religion. It is a place of forms, of life, of shadows. It is, in psychological terms, the unconscious, the land of anxiety or bliss, our most familiar inner haunt.

And upward through the body of our muse, our loved one, comes the real world, the outside world. Our muse, our lover, has became transparent, the membrane inside is breached, the limits of time and space come back, and we are in body land, the material world. And here things are equally surreal, but are more familiar to doctors. The lands we have just left were the painter's realms, these lands are the physician's. So what do we have here in the land of the medical center? First the mind, consciousness, thinking. Here are thoughts, emotions, images. They form in different areas of the brain, involve various neurotransmitters, the firing of neurons, the lighting up of areas of the brain as we love, and make art, and soar, and feel. And those firing neurons, those nets of cascading activity, connect to the body in three simple ways.

First the right brain, the home of imagery, sends messages to the lower brain areas which connect to the hypothalamus. This area activates the autonomic nervous system and results in arousal or relaxation of a double balancing system that reaches out to the whole body and touches virtually every cell. The sympathetic branch is the branch of fight and flight, the running from the tiger, the defensive posture. So, an image of threat in the brain alerts the hypothalamus to cause sympathetic arousal, and this speeds up the heartbeat, increases breathing, sends blood to the large muscles, floods the body with adrenaline and hormones, and creates a physiology of alertness. The stimulation of the parasympathetic nervous system results in relaxation, in healing, in maintenance. Heartbeat and blood pressure slow, breathing slows, blood goes to the intestines, all changes. We now have the physiology of healing, of creativity. This oversimplified model gives us a gross idea of how the mind is connected to the body.

Second we have the hormonal flood that bathes every cell in the body as the imagery of threat or love lights up the neural nets in the big brain. As the light flashes through our brain, the hypothalamus sends messages to the adrenal glands to release epinepherine, adrenaline and other hormones which travel throughout the body and are picked up by receptors on our cells and cause some cells to contract, others to relax, some to act, others to rest. So our entire physiology is changed a second time by an image held in our brain, our consciousness, and to it we respond.

Finally we enter the realm of the neurotransmitter. Images in the brain cause specific areas of the brain itself to release endorphins and other neurotransmitters which effect brain cells and cells of the immune system. The neurotransmitters relieve pain and make the immune system function more efficiently. They make killer cells eat cancer cells, white blood cells attack AIDS viruses and generally change the body's ability to respond to illness.

So what do we have here? We are in the midst of a modern myth that basically says that a thought changes a cell which helps us heal. Three steps: 1) the thought; 2) the message to the cells, a nerve impulse, a hormone, or a neurotransmitter; 3) the cells' response—eating a cancer cell or virus, or relaxing or tensing. This is a simple myth. It is biological, physical, in the flesh. It tries to connect the mind and body which are still seen as separate, but at least speaking to each other. It does not view the body as an automaton uninfluenced by thoughts and perceptions. The evolution of this myth took a half-century and was a great step in modern science. It broke the separation of mind and body, the Cartesian split that ruled science and even psychology for a century and prevented life from entering medicine.

So, with this oversimplified three step model in mind, let's drift gently back to the real world. How did that model make you feel—safe, stolid, bored, confused, science ignorant, grounded, cold? It certainly is not elevating for me, but it is necessary to see as a base of belief, a connection between the worlds of science and the worlds of art. So let's drift back into art, (this is an art show, not a medical conference), let's feel again how art opens our hearts and relate that to the three step model. Just trying this for a moment tells me that there is something dreadfully wrong with the whole thing. As I close my eyes and feel my heart opening, as I see my wife dying of breast cancer before me and feel her love, as I hear a song of love enter our hospital room and see the art that surrounded us there in our sacred space, our shrine of rebirth, the three step model just doesn't hold water. It is a flimsy basket, a vessel crafted for another purpose.

So here is another model, one from contemporary psychology that comes a little closer to how I actually feel inside. Remember, this too, is just a scaffold, a structure to try to explain the ineffable, to try to put a foundation under us as we undertake this exciting journey.

I see our bodies as an aggregate of matter attracted by an idea. The idea has no independent existence, it is a part of the whole, and also of the individual, of our body. From far within, from the reaches of the deepest space this idea has grown, formed, reformed and changed. It is now you or me and is moving forward still faster and faster. If we go deep into the darkness, far back, way back, downward, downward, we reach the place of no return, the home, the genesis. There, from there, flows our soul, our spirit, the first manifestation of this light, the first light itself. And from the darkness, wholeness, where there is no beginning or end, no time and little space, the soul grows, expands, and enters the idea and is with mind and body for a while. Body/mind/spirit is an aggregate, an entity, a being. This being is you or me and is integral, whole and one and is at the same time connected, of, embedded, is.

The body's health depends on its balance, its physiology. When its systems are in order, blood flows at a certain pressure, the heart beats at a certain rate, the hormones are in a certain balance. I now see this balance as coming from a dialogue of body/mind/spirit. I see the spirit awakening, being awake, being listened to, talking to the mind/body. It tells the mind/body both through the body's feelings and tension levels, and through the mind's feelings, emotions, images and thoughts, how to balance. When the spirit is not heeded, imbalance results. This feels like discomfort. When the spirit is heeded, the body/mind/spirit resonates, it dances and sings, it comes alive as a unit and healing happens.

And here we must speak of energy. When you talk of healing, when you experience healing, you feel energy. When we talk of a resonation of body/mind/spirit we mean a freeing of energy, a resonation of the life force, a buzzing, tingling, flow, a vibration, a hovering. And the energy is felt as a sensation, a feeling, it can flow throughout the body, from body to body, from the universe to us. It can be seen by psychics and meditators, and can be portrayed in art. What is this energy, chi, prana, kundalini, Gods' breath, acupuncture energy meridians, chakras, the life force? It has been described throughout all time; it is an integral part of the human experience. Because art acts at the level of the spirit, because art is the language of the spirit, energy is involved. Perhaps the simplest metaphor for how art heals is that it frees our body's healing energy to flow. The spirit sees the image, the spirit soars, goes home, unites with the deep source, and energy is released like a torrent, like a breakthrough, like a waterfall.

The bringing home releases energy. That is all.

How does healing occur? The resonating body/mind/spirit balances the body's physiology by the threefold path we mentioned above: thoughts in the brain; autonomic nervous system balance, hormonal balance, and neurotransmitter balance; and cellular change. So my theory, although it sounds more mystical, is really the same as the other one—with a difference. It postulates the existence of the third element, the spirit or soul. Why do this? Why have religions, mystics, artists, and healers done this for all recorded history, why is this exhibition called "Body and Soul?" The only answer I can come to is that it more accurately matches our actual experience than a model devoid of spirit—it seems true. As I write this essay I struggle to bring to light my deepest feelings, to express in words what I sense below words. This is the work of the artist, the mystic, the healer—the making real, bringing to light, manifesting of the sounds that are too subtle to be heard in the tumult, the singing of the soul.

And as I have said, the spirit or soul speaks to the body/mind through the language of art. It is that simple. Below art, the soul speaks in the language of the long breath, of the pause between breaths, of inner peace, of the place below images and sound, the *om.* Resting there is rest. Resting there is peace. Resting there is home. But the next place is art, the next place is the birth of the image.

What are these things called images and how are they related to art? Images are thoughts that come in the form of experiences. They have the shape of the sensory modalities that feed them. They are in real time in that they are touch, sound, sight, smell, and taste and are beyond real time in that they can glimpse realms that cannot be felt with senses. They are different from thought in that they have shape. Unlike a math problem or worry, images are not made of words unless they are cloaked in poetry. They do not flow as language directly unless they are made of inner speech, complicated.

Psychologists divide imagery into several categories which help us understand what they mean by images. Memory images are images of events that took place in the past; imagination images are not based on discrete events from the outer world. Dream images were experienced in sleep, hypnopompic images upon awakening, hypnagogic images while going to sleep. Visions are images experienced while awake or in a trance that are vivid. Hallucinations are images experienced while awake that are poorly controllable. Vividness and controllability are terms that show us how psychologists describe the imagery experience. When the experience of imagery is intense, when the images are bright, loud, or very attention-getting, they are vivid. When images are unbidden, cannot be gotten rid of, or cannot be changed, they are poorly controllable.

I divide imagery into two basic types—receptive and programmed. Receptive imagery comes to you, it arrives on the scene, bidden or unbidden, and rests in your mind's eye. It can come into a blank screen and appear as itself, or it can come over your thoughts and appear mixed. You may know that the image has arrived, or you may suspect it has from how you feel. Programmed imagery is different. You choose an image and hold it in your thoughts for a reason. The choice may be deliberate or you may choose an image that came to you from the receptive space. Either way the image effects your world.

How does the image effect your world? It effects your body by the threefold path; first an image in the right brain, next messages to the autonomic nervous system, the adrenal glands, the neurotransmitters. Finally, each cell in your body is changed. Images effect your world by giving you ideas to plan from, emotional motivation to continue, and meaning to free energy. When a person gets an image of the future, he or she then can make it happen. Magic is the image becoming real in the outer world.

How do healers work with imagery? The most common technique involves having patients picture their illness, their healing forces, and the healing process in the mind's eye. First, the patients imagine what the illness looks like in as much detail as they can. Next, they imagine how the body's resources could deal with the visualized illness. This is imagined as a process over time. For example, patients picture cancer cells, picture them in an area of the body, picture them as a certain color, shape, smell, texture. They then picture killer cells or white blood cells eating the cancer cells. They picture the body's defenses advancing, multiplying, engulfing the cells whole and wiping them all out. This biological imagery is most effective if it is anatomically accurate and detailed. Researchers have found that if this imagery is very specific, for example if one type of white blood cell is pictured, it alone is found to rise in blood counts. Next patients are encouraged to allow metaphorical imagery to form. For example, they imagine little men, dogs, or white light blasting, eating, or dissolving blackness, mud, or other little men. Generally this metaphorical imagery takes place spontaneously after the biological imagery. Finally, patients hold a programmed image in mind. They picture themselves healed, surrounded by white light, surrounded by energy, as a God, as a power animal or as strong and secure. In this show, Nancy Burson's visualizations supply imagery for the first type of biological imagery healing. Alex Grey's and C. Regina Kelley's images can be held in mind for programmed imagery healing.

So, healing art can be used by a patient in two obvious ways. The images can be viewed and the balancing nature of them can be allowed to change a person's consciousness, or images can be used to help a person visualize the healing process or a healed state. In both of these types of healing, the art provides imagery seen by the artist. The imagery heals if it relaxes, puts patients in an altered state, opens their hearts, or moves them and gives them energy. Monet's *Water Lilies* are so relaxing for most people that patients often visit museums and sit and meditate in front of them for hours.

The third way art heals a viewer is by showing patients images that move them. When patients with breast cancer see Nancy Fried's sculpture, it opens them up to emotions they may have hidden. This allows them to discuss these emotions with family, support people, and their healers. Patients who have a particular illness are moved by art that portrays other patients' experiences with the same illness. It makes them feel connected, relieves isolation, and releases deep emotions. This type of art can be very disturbing for other people to view. The imagery, often gory or graphic, is not for relaxation or transcendence—it is for opening the heart.

Therefore, for the healing artist, there are several types of healing art: relaxing, balancing images whose presence is transformative by themselves, images of pain that are moving, and biological images that provide a library of images to visualize. All these types of healing art are powerful and effective. They all work by changing consciousness, by freeing energy, by awakening the spirit to resonate body/mind/spirit. They are the technology of healing art, its tools, its machines. When art is made by the patient, similar types of art do similar things. But the imagery can be more powerful because it comes from the inner world of the person who is ill. The imagery is more direct, more meaningful and sometimes more effective. However the images made by artists can be so powerful, so filled with energy, that even though they are not personal to the patient, they too can be transformative.

Throughout recorded history, artists have believed that their images have power in themselves. Shamanic art was believed to actually have the power to change the physical world. Its shape and color were believed to be powerful, to be able to transmit and move real energy. Just standing near a piece of healing art was believed to be a healing experience. No viewing was necessary, no understanding obligatory, just an experience that brought about molecular change. This concept is difficult for many Westerners to grasp scientifically, but it is not foreign from our lives. People carry good luck charms, relics, holy objects. People make shrines, sacred spaces, churches and meditation rooms. Patients surround themselves with power animals, religious talismans and crystals. The belief in the healing energy of objects is deep even in our rational logical world.

Artists have worked with their images for all recorded history. In fact, during its infancy, recorded history was just that. Artists saw, felt, heard, touched, smelled or tasted something in their mind's eye and then brought it out into the world as a material form or reproduction of the image. This process occurred consciously or unconsciously, the image was birthed from an image that was glimpsed or from an intuition that there was something there that had to be expressed. This conscious or unconscious evocation of imagery results in two techniques of making healing art.

In unconscious healing art, the artist knows that an image must be freed, and lets it come. He or she sees the art work unfolding and knows whether it is right or wrong.

"Erase that, that isn't right. That's it." In conscious healing art, the artist meditates, sees an image and brings it out. The production of the art is an act of seeing more clearly, looking at the image and the art, and cross-checking it over and over again. "Is that right, no we need more light coming out of that hole."

Healing art is being born as we speak. The concept is catching fire and awakening in peoples' spirits. The idea is being born anew. It is being born in two worlds simultaneously. In the world of the artist, artists are realizing that their imagery has meaning. They are understanding that their imagery heals them, others, their neighborhood, or the earth. This realization does not come easily. It comes in a flash, as an awakening. It comes in spite of the art community, it is inevitable. When artists make healing images they feel such energy around them that they cannot help but make more. Their lives are changed, their world is changed. The second vision comes from the world of the healer. Art in the hospital, or art at the bedside with a person who is ill, is an electrifying experience. It becomes the doorway for the spirit and the vehicle for the opening of the heart. It is integral to healing.

How does this rebirth of art and healing manifest itself in the outer world? First there are now artists making healing art purposely. It is a new field in art. This art, as I see it, heals the self, another, or the world. When the artist makes art, and feels better, it heals. This art heals by freeing the artist's own healing energy and resonating the body/mind/spirit. Second, the artist can make a piece of art to heal another person. The artist can do it specifically for one person or for a group of people. It is transpersonal healing, it connects one to another, it is an art of interconnection. It is from the oneness. It joins us at our centers. Thus art heals by releasing the energies of viewers, relaxing them, allowing something within them to be freed, again resonating the body/mind/spirit. Finally the third type of art heals the world. The artist makes a piece that works with the energy of a whole system, whether it be a neighborhood, an ecosystem, or the planet itself. This art can be ceremonial, environmental, performed, or static. It involves the community. It involves energy and movement. It is truly shamanic, it balances the world.

When patients make art to heal, with or without a guide, or when patients experience art in their healing, we have the second broad category of healing art. Art at the bedside, art workshops for patients, art therapy, art exhibitions at hospitals and environments in healing centers, all represent this type.

Do you want to feel healing energy, experience healing art? When you walk through this show, open your heart. Imagine that you or a loved one is ill and needs love. Let yourself be deeply moved by Nancy Fried's chilling images. Stop, rest there, feel their sorrow, let the sorrow within you come out. Feel Khristine Hopkins's images of abuse and healing. Feel the differences between the two spaces. Allow your emotions to surface, open your heart, feel abuse, feel healing. Journey into Denise Bardovi's stellar work. Be her for a moment. Imagine how she discovered the enemy, the virus. Feel her shaman healer arrive. Look at her transformation, feel its peace and beauty. Let Alex Grey's images slip into your consciousness, feel the energy in his lines and dots. Imagine you are the God he portrays, he has seen. Feel the flames as power. Let your body be a receiver for his message. Now let any thoughts of illness flow out of you. Let light flow in. Be healed. Feel the power within you rise, feel your center strengthen. Rest in the moments between your breaths.

This is not a passive art form. Healing art is not meant to be merely watched. This is the life force. This art is made to change reality. This art has the power to transform. We are on the doorstep of a great journey. This show is one of its beginnings. Imagine where we can go. Imagine art in every hospital, art with anyone who is ill. Imagine lifting the spirits of someone who is about to die. Imagine being in love.

Mike Samuels is a California physician who has conducted research, lectured, and written extensively on visualization in medicine and healing. His many books include *The Well Body Book,* co-authored with Hal Bennett, and *Seeing with the Mind's Eye* and *The Well Baby Book,* both co-authored with his late wife, Nancy Samuels.

CHECKLIST OF THE EXHIBITION

All works are lent by the artist unless otherwise noted. Dimensions are in inches; height precedes width precedes depth.

Eric Avery (Texas)

Barney Clarke Meets Baby Fae on the Road to Africa, from the "American Medicine" series, 1985,
wood engraving
Courtesy Mary Ryan Gallery, New York, NY

Kaposi's Sarcoma (A),
printed in collaboration with Robert Townsend, 1993,
linocut with monotype,
24 1/2 x 19
Courtesy Mary Ryan Gallery, New York, NY

Kaposi's Sarcoma (B),
printed in collaboration with Robert Townsend, 1993,
linocut with monotype,
24 1/2 x 19
Courtesy Mary Ryan Gallery, New York, NY

The Last Lymphocyte (A),
printed in collaboration with Robert Townsend, 1993,
linocut with monotype,
24 1/2 x 19
Courtesy Mary Ryan Gallery, New York, NY

The Last Lymphocyte (B),
printed in collaboration with Robert Townsend, 1993,
linocut with monotype,
24 1/2 x 19
Courtesy Mary Ryan Gallery, New York, NY

The Medical Student of the Future, from the "American Medicine" series, 1985,
wood engraving
Courtesy Mary Ryan Gallery, New York, NY

The Modern Tumble Into Life, from the "American Medicine" series, 1985,
wood engraving
Courtesy Mary Ryan Gallery, New York, NY

Neonatal Manger Scene, from the "American Medicine" series, 1985,
wood engraving
Courtesy Mary Ryan Gallery, New York, NY

Small Pox (A),
printed in collaboration with Robert Townsend,
linocut with monotype,
24 1/2 x 19
Courtesy Mary Ryan Gallery, New York, NY

Small Pox (B),
printed in collaboration with Robert Townsend,
linocut with monotype,
24 1/2 x 19
Courtesy Mary Ryan Gallery, New York, NY

The Stuff of Life, 1993,
reduction linocut on handmade Japanese Okawara paper,
cast paper woodcut spheres,
73 x 37 (each sheet),
12 (diameter of spheres)
Courtesy Mary Ryan Gallery, New York, NY

Denise Bardovi (California)

#9, Never Again, 1986,
tempera on paper, 26 x 20

#10, Self Portrait #1, 1986,
tempera on paper, 57 x 20

#11, Back in L.A., 1986,
tempera on paper, 26 x 20

#12, Mother Earth, 1986,
tempera on paper, 26 x 20

#13, The Virus, 1986,
tempera on paper, 26 x 20

#14, Panic Attack on Paper, 1986,
tempera on paper, 26 x 20

#16, The Shaman #2, 1986,
tempera on paper, 26 x 20

#17, Dying, 1986,
tempera on paper, 26 x 20

#25, Sun Spirit, 1986,
tempera on paper, 26 x 20

Nancy Burson (New York)

Visualization image for AIDS related pneumonia, 1988,
Type C print,
16 1/4 x 20 1/4
Courtesy of the Jayne H. Baum Gallery, New York, NY

Visualization image for breast cancer, 1989,
Type C print,
16 1/4 x 20 1/4
Courtesy of the Jayne H. Baum Gallery, New York, NY

Visualization image for cervical cancer, 1989,
Type C print,
16 1/4 x 20 1/4
Courtesy of the Jayne H. Baum Gallery, New York, NY

Visualization image for leukemia, 1989,
Type C print,
16 1/4 x 20 1/4
Courtesy of the Jayne H. Baum Gallery, New York, NY

Visualization image for lung cancer, 1989,
Type C print,
16 1/4 x 20 1/4
Courtesy of the Jayne H. Baum Gallery, New York, NY

Visualize This, poster, 1991,
17 3/4 x 29

Christiane Corbat (Rhode Island)

Amazon, Cry for Life, 1989,
plaster fabric, wasp nest, feathers, aluminum,
18 x 17 x 10

Amazon, the Offering, 1988–89,
plaster fabric, paint, flax, burlap,
39 x 25 x 5

Chrysalis, 1991,
plaster fabric, wasp nest, wood, animal intestine, earth,
26 x 35 x 24

Kiva Woman, 1993,
plaster fabric, paint, feathers, fox fur, brass fittings, wood,
35 x 16 x 15

Placental Bloom, 1990,
plaster fabric, burlap, paint, feathers, alpaca wool, wasp nest, wood, brass, earth,
46 x 18 x 14

Nancy Fried (New York)

Breast Ex-Voto, 1987,
terra cotta, 6 1/2 x 2 1/4 x 3 1/2

The Flirt, 1987,
terra cotta, 10 1/2 x 13 x 5

The Hand Mirror, 1987,
terra cotta, 10 x 9 1/2 x 8

Hanging Out, 1987,
terra cotta, 10 x 9 1/2 x 8,
Private Collection

In Memory of 1986–1987, 1987,
terra cotta, 8 1/2 x 7 1/2 x 9,
Collection of the Honorable Judge Herbert Fogel

Mourning, 1987,
terra cotta, 8 1/2 x 4 1/2 x 3 1/2

Still the Nightmare, 1987,
terra cotta, 10 x 9 1/2 x 8,
Collection of the Honorable Judge Herbert Fogel

The Unkept Secret, 1987,
terra cotta, 9 1/2 x 8 3/4 x 6,
Collection of Kathryn Weill

Alex Grey (New York)

Dying, 1990,
oil on linen,
60 x 44
Collection of Bex Frankel

Journey of the Wounded Healer,
triptych, 1984–1985,
oil on linen,
90 x 216
Collection of the Museum of Contemporary Art, San Diego;
Gift of Linda and Stefan Stux

Marcy Hermansader (Vermont)

After, 1988,
color pencil, spray paint, acrylic and gold foil on paper,
20 1/4 x 20

Alterations in the Blood, 1985,
color pencil, acrylic, and fabric on paper,
30 x 18

Geology of Emotion,
color pencil, acrylic, foil, and fabric on paper,
26 x 18
Collection of Nessa Theo Rosen

Touch and Feel, 1986,
color pencil and acrylic on paper,
24 1/4 x 18
Collection of Walter and Wendy Foulke

Transfusion, 1988,
color pencil, spray paint, acrylic, fabric, foil on paper,
31 1/2 x 39 1/2
DeCordova Museum Permanent Collection; gift of Jonathan Flaccus

Khristine Hopkins (Massachusetts)

#3— Mary, 1990,
photograph hand-painted with oil paint, 7 x 4 5/8

#16— Mary, 1990,
photograph hand-painted with oil paint, 4 5/8 x 7

#6— Khristine, 1990,
photograph hand-painted with oil paint, 4 5/8 x 7

#14— Khristine, 1990,
photograph hand-painted with oil paint, 4 5/8 x 7

#9— Yvonne, 1990,
photograph hand-painted with oil paint, 7 x 4 5/8

#12— Yvonne, 1990,
photograph hand-painted with oil paint, 4 5/8 x 7

C. Regina Kelley (Maine)

Quan Yin, 1993, 60 (diameter),
ceramic

Riva Lehrer (Illinois)

Bodice, 1992,
acrylic on metal and wood,
14 x 12
Courtesy of Sazama Gallery, Chicago, IL

Chorus, 1993,
acrylic on masonite,
5 x 7
Courtesy of Sazama Gallery, Chicago, IL

Diagnosis II, 1992,
acrylic on panel,
6 x 5 3/4
Courtesy of Sazama Gallery, Chicago, IL

In the Yellow Woods, 1994,
acrylic on masonite,
8 x 10
Courtesy of Sazama Gallery, Chicago, IL

Tim Lowly (Illinois)

Beacon ("Bless the Bastard"), 1991,
tempera on panel,
48 x 60

Beacon (Kite), 1991,
tempera on panel,
7 x 7
Collection of Warren B. and Anne Weisberg

Face of the Deep, 1989,
tempera with mixed media,
15 x 50

If, 1992,
tempera, 3 x 3

Imago Dei, 1991,
ink on paper, 22 x 15

Maggie McCurdy (New Mexico)

Cell Stream 5, 1989,
acrylic and mixed media on canvas,
38 1/2 x 42 1/2

Cell Stream 7, 1990,
acrylic and mixed media on canvas,
60 x 84

Cell Stream 8, 1991,
acrylic and mixed media on canvas,
46 1/2 x 56

Untitled, 1989,
acrylic and mixed media on canvas,
41 1/2 x 56

Catherine Nash (Arizona)

Under Twilight's Dream, 1994,
handmade flax and abaca paper walls, sprayed pulp, branches, pine needles, silver leaf, dimensions variable within room size of
13 x 16 x 16 feet

David Schorr (New York)

Achates, 1993,
silverpoint, toned gesso with gouache and acrylic on linen,
10 x 18
Courtesy Mary Ryan Gallery, New York, NY

Body, Remember, 1993,
silverpoint, toned gesso with acrylic and gold leaf on linen,
26 x 20
Courtesy Mary Ryan Gallery, New York, NY

Ceaseless Rain, 1993,
silverpoint, toned gesso with gouache and acrylic on linen,
14 x 26
Courtesy Mary Ryan Gallery, New York, NY

Dance of Death, 1991,
lithograph, four colors from plates on Moriki paper,
26 x 19
Courtesy Mary Ryan Gallery, New York, NY

Death &, 1993,
lithograph, four colors,
(one stone and three plates)
on Moulin de Fleurac paper,
26 x 20
Courtesy Mary Ryan Gallery, New York, NY

Easeful Death, 1991,
lithograph, three colors (1 blended roll) from plates on BFK paper,
30 x 22
Courtesy Mary Ryan Gallery, New York, NY

Little Soul, 1992,
silverpoint, toned gesso with gouache and acrylic on linen,
11 x 20
Courtesy Mary Ryan Gallery, New York, NY

Soldiers, 1992,
silverpoint, leadpoint, toned gesso with gouache and acrylic on linen,
14 x 26
Courtesy Mary Ryan Gallery, New York, NY

Vanished Summer, 1993,
lithograph, four color (one stone and three plates) on Moulin de Fleurac paper,
26 x 20
Courtesy Mary Ryan Gallery, New York, NY

Ann Leda Shapiro (Washington)

Cells, 1992,
watercolor, 22 x 34

Inside, 1990,
watercolor, 18 x 36

Intestine, 1992,
watercolor, 24 x 36

Neuron, 1988,
watercolor, 40 x 15

No, 1992,
watercolor, 30 x 22

Hollis Sigler (Illinois)

Fear Like A Cancer Was Eating Her Up, 1992,
oil pastel on paper with painted frame,
38 1/2 x 28 1/2
Collection of Pat Pinkerton and Art Wieland; Courtesy Steven Scott Gallery, Baltimore, MD

Maybe It Was in Something I Ate, 1992,
oil pastel on paper with painted frame,
34 x 29
Collection of Mr. Charles Vonderheid; Courtesy Steven Scott Gallery, Baltimore, MD

Trying to Maintain an Air of Normalcy, 1992,
oil pastel on paper with painted frame,
34 x 29
Collection of Jean Howard and Joseph Virde

When She Lost Control She Only Wanted It Back, 1992,
oil pastel on paper with painted frame,
34 x 29
Collection of Jean Howard and Joseph Virde

Beth Ames Swartz (New York)

Chakra #1—Base of the Spine from "A Moving Point of Balance," 1983,
gold leaf and mixed media on linen, 84 x 84
Collection of Stanton Perry

Chakra #3—Solar Plexus from "A Moving Point of Balance," 1984,
microglitter and mixed media on linen, 84 x 84
Collection of Stanton Perry

Chakra #6- Third Eye from "A Moving Point of Balance," 1985,
microglitter and mixed media on linen, 84 x 84
Collection of Stanton Perry

Ottie Thomas-Smith (Maine)

Artificial eye, 1994,
acrylic, 1 x 2

Auricular prosthesis, 1994,
silicone, 3 x 2

Facial cast of patient with prosthesis, 1994,
silicone, 8 x 5

Facial cast of patient without prosthesis, 1994,
silicone, 8 x 5

Nasal prosthesis, 1994,
silicone, 3 x 2

Orbital prosthesis, 1994,
silicone, 4 x 5

Linda Troeller (New York)

Baden Baden, Germany, 1991,
Type C print, 20 x 24

Evian Spa, Evian France, Mother/Father/Baby Program, 1989,
Type C print, 20 x 24

Jacuzzi, Calistoga Hot Springs, California, 1992,
Type C print, 20 x 24

Men's Pool, Ojo Caliente, New Mexico, 1990,
Type C print, 20 x 24

Mud, Dead Sea, 1990,
Type C print, 20 x 24

Steam, Carson Hot Springs, Nevada, 1991,
Type C print, 20 x 24